CODI'S JOURNEY

An Inspiring and Heartwarming Story
About an Amazing Best Friend

Jeff Maziarek

SpiritSimple Enterprises L.L.C.
Villa Park, Illinois
www.codipup.com

Published by:
SpiritSimple Enterprises L.L.C.
P.O. Box 6973
Villa Park, IL 60181

First Edition:

eBook version – December 2010

Print on Demand book – May 2011

Draft desktop publishing and PDF generation services by Lisa Rash

Cover design by Chris Hansen (chansen4817@comcast.net)

Design services for printed book by Barbara Dufford at Big Picture Design (bigpicturedesign.blogspot.com) (bdufford@sbcglobal.net)

The author wishes to express his appreciation to the artist listed below for her kind permission to print her copyrighted material:

Roseann Romeo-Maziarek, for her poem *Codi's Gift* © 2006 and her artwork *Codi Image* © 1994. All rights reserved. Reproduced by permission of the artist.

Published by arrangement with the author.

ISBN 978-0-9744841-3-6

Printed in the United States of America.

10 9 8 7 6 5 4 3 2

For reprint permissions or other information, address the Permissions Department, SpiritSimple Enterprises L.L.C., P.O. Box 6973, Villa Park, IL, 60181. E-mail: codi@codipup.com

This book is dedicated to:

Codi, for her unconditional love and
amazing spiritual insights

Andrea, for her enduring love, friendship,
and steadfast support

The late *Rick Clark,* for his more than forty years
of loyal friendship

Table of Contents

Acknowledgments

Bringing *Codi's Journey* from concept to paper would not have occurred without support and assistance from a number of people. My most heartfelt gratitude goes out to:

Angel Gail Konz and *Lisa Jacobsen*, for giving me the initial inspiration to write this book

Pam Sourelis, for sharing her amazing animal communication skills at critically important times during Codi's final year

Dr. Laura Clarke, for her loving and compassionate care of Codi

The late *Rick Clark*, for over four decades of friendship and for taking such excellent care of our dog Heidi during our lengthy trips to Greece in 2006 and 2007. Without his willingness to uproot his life and move into our home for several weeks each of those summers, it's quite possible I might never have completed this book.

Debby and *Carley Clegg*, for their compassionate and loving care of both Codi and Heidi over the years

The late *Renee Chadwick*, for being my very best pal and sounding board

The late *Laura Hansen*, for her friendship, consistent encouragement, and spiritual support

Peter Cunningham, for providing expert proofreading assistance on the final first draft manuscript and *Elaine Cunningham*, for her friendship and support of my work

Noreene Damolaris, for always taking the time to really listen to me and truly be there for me whenever I've needed her

Lisa Rash, for her expert desktop publishing assistance and valuable creative input, and equally as important, for her friendship

Pete Koerner, author of *The Belief Formula*, (www.thebeliefor-mula.com), his amazing wife Jen, and *Gloria Wendroff*, author of *Heavenletters*, (www.heavenletters.org) for their ongoing support and encouragement

John Pfeuffer, for patronizing my technical writing business throughout the time this book was being written and well beyond

Chris Hansen, for his beautiful book cover design, his valuable writing insights, and for content-related input on the final manuscript

Roseann Romeo-Maziarek, for her moving poem, *Codi's Gift,* and for her beautiful illustration of Codi

Barbara Dufford, of *Big Picture Design* (bigpicturedesign.blogspot.com), for her exceptional, value-added design and layout of the print version of *Codi's Journey*

Carol Adler, (www.caroladler.com) for her sage advice about writing and publishing

Paul Burt, (www.penandpublish.com) for so generously sharing his time and publishing expertise

Jan Martin and *Mike Maziarek* for being the best sister and brother a guy could want

Gary Madden, for three decades of friendship and for being an ongoing source of encouragement

Sandra Golatte, for her support of this work, and for her daily reminders for me to keep working on it

Sandra Cisneros, for her friendship and generosity in providing me with emotional and physical healing support when I needed it most

Eileen Oeser, for her support and encouragement throughout the course of this project

Bill Lewis and *Ron Mangelsdorf* of The Quest Group for their generosity in allowing me to print and bind numerous manuscript copies of this book at their expense

In addition, I want to express my sincere appreciation to the following people who all took the time to read and provide content-related input on the complete final first draft manuscript: *Carol Adler, Joanne Berridge, Teresa Betcher, Steve Dale, Kristen Damolaris, Steven Damolaris, Pegi DeMeo, Terry DiPadova, Sandra Golatte, Rob Graff, Babette Herman, Katie Griffith, Pete Koerner, Bette Krebel, Eugenia Last, Mary Lou Meader, Michele McKenzie, Therese Mohar, Joyce Naylor, Sharee Pemberton,*

Dan Price, Susan Ross, Todd Savitt, Sara Sgarlat, Neil Story, Teresa Tharp, Gloria Wendroff, and *Terri Wernert*

Finally, I say a hearty thank you to:

Nathalie Yonow, for her generosity in granting me the use of one of her family's houses while writing on the Greek island of Alonnisos for the entire summer of 2007

Nectarios Florous of the Kastro Restaurant in Alonnisos, for his friendship, and for his hospitality and kindness during my stay on the island

Chester and *Sarah Smith,* for their amazing hospitality, and for their thoughtfulness in inviting me to join the sing-along sessions at the Aloni Taverna in Alonnisos

Susan and *Alan Ross,* for their encouragement, and spiritual advice and counsel during my stay on Alonnisos in 2007

Eleni Papachristou of the *Flisvos Estiatorio,* and *Eleni Anagnostou,* owner of *Anais Cafe,* for being so incredibly friendly and hospitable to me while I was writing on Alonnisos

Ria and *Yiannis Anagnostou* of the *Megalo Mourtia Taverna,* for being so welcoming and gracious to me during my writing time on Alonnisos

Introduction

If you've selected this book, I can safely assume that at some point in your life you have had the pleasure of sharing your home and life with a dog (or dogs). Perhaps you've been close to dogs your whole life, or maybe it's only more recently you've discovered the joy of having canines around. Either way, it's likely you and I share a deep and abiding affection for them.

In my case, the earliest recollection I have of interacting with dogs dates back to the spring of 1968 when my best friend's dog had a litter of puppies. Even though I was 11 years old at the time, this was actually the first opportunity I ever had to see and play with such little pups. In the few weeks that followed that initial visit, I would come to spend many hours there having fun with them and just reveling in their love and attention. Eventually, I became fascinated with a particular black and white female who always paid me more mind than any of the others. She wound up joining our family in June of that year after my mother finally gave in to my constant pleading.

Since that time over four decades ago, I've had one or more dogs sharing a home with me for nearly 35 of those years. While each of these dogs genuinely touched my heart, it was Codi, a certain feisty little Border Collie, who affected me most deeply. Not only was she my *best friend* in every sense of the term, she also turned out to be an amazing spiritual teacher. While some might scoff at the idea that a dog could actually *teach* anything to an intellectually superior human being, the truth is intelligence is just one aspect of any creature's abilities. The dog's unwavering loyalty, its unique ability to live totally in the present and its unmatched capacity to give unconditional love, even under the most challenging of circumstances, truly makes it an ideal spiritual role model.

From early on in my relationship with Codi, I always felt that beneath the fur there was a very sentient being. And, in the last year of our time together some very *mystical* events ultimately transpired to completely confirm the accuracy of that feeling. In this book I explain each of these events within the context of a detailed narrative describing the very challenging journey Codi faced during the final 12 months of her life. To provide even deeper insight into her story, I also detail how she came to be a part of our family and I share many engaging anecdotes about her personality and some of her more memorable deeds over the years.

My foremost intention in telling this story is to share two key messages. First, that our pets (dogs in this instance), actually are "sages with fur" who have a far greater understanding of life (and us) than commonly thought. Second, that it's perfectly normal to feel intense and long-lasting grief at the loss of a pet. This is particularly so when that animal served as one's primary companion for many years. In this regard, I sincerely want any reader who also has experienced such a loss to know that someone truly does understand the sadness and emptiness they felt when their beloved pet passed on. Finally, it's my hope that such readers come to understand how important it is to fully process their feelings of grief by really *feeling* them, rather than keeping them locked up inside.

If after reading *Codi's Journey* you have any comments or questions regarding the book, please feel free to contact me by referring to the Author Contact page located at the back.

Thanks for your interest in this work!

1. April 12, 2004

As the spring of 2004 arrived, it became very apparent that our Border Collie, Codi (or "the BC" as we often referred to her), had lost some weight over the winter. This was very unusual. Typically, our dogs tended to put on some pounds during previous winter seasons due to their reduced outdoor activity. Initially we didn't think much of it since, during a trip to the veterinarian in February for her annual shots, the doctor didn't raise any flags about her weight. Moreover, her appetite certainly hadn't changed and her energy level was essentially as high as ever, even though she had just turned twelve years old.

Codi, like most Border Collies, was always a very active dog, one that literally demanded to play (also known as work) several times a day. If you're not familiar with this breed, words cannot adequately describe just how committed these dogs are to their work and how intensely they focus on it. If you've actually had one in your life then you know exactly what I'm talking about. Simply put, Border Collies are not the type of dog to leave alone all day without something to keep them occupied, as they actually crave activities that challenge them both physically and mentally.

While visiting my brother's house for Easter dinner, we mentioned Codi's weight loss to my sister-in-law, Roseann, an avid animal lover. Her response was a strong recommendation to take the BC to the vet as soon as possible. She stressed that, as with humans, weight loss in a pet can be indicative of a serious medical condition. While I clearly heard what she said, I chose not to focus on it, primarily because Codi had, for the most part, been a very healthy dog her whole life. This, combined with the fact that in my spiritual growth process I learned the importance of not giving thought or feeling energy to what I *didn't want*, caused me to hesitate in calling the vet early the very next day to make an appointment. Looking back, I suppose there also was a bit of "denial" operating within me, because, at some level, I refused to believe my beloved animal soul mate could actually have contracted a serious illness.

This attitude didn't last very long. Even though I was doing my best to apply positive thinking to the situation, my gut-level instincts were telling me Codi's health was indeed at risk. Nonetheless, before calling the vet the next morning I decided to check in with my dear friend Lisa Jacobsen, a very gifted energy healer[1], who has uncanny skills as a "medical intuitive." If you're unfamiliar with this skill, individuals who possess it have the ability to recognize patterns of illnesses within people or animals without any need to actually be in the same room, town, state, or country for that matter. In essence, they are able to psychically tune in to the patient's energy field[2] and intuitively see/feel if there is an energy blockage that either has the potential to lead to the development of some type of disease, or which already has. Perhaps the most renowned medical intuitive in the U.S. today is Caroline Myss, who has written numerous books about healing and has been an occasional guest on The Oprah Show.

In any event, when I phoned Lisa on Monday afternoon she could noticeably sense I was in some emotional distress about the situation. Out of the kindness of her heart, she offered to take a few moments to "look into" Codi's energy field. After the phone went quiet for a minute or so, Lisa returned to say that she sensed some type of irregular cell growth on the left side of her liver near the edge of the rib cage. In that moment my heart literally sank, and I quickly asked, "When you say *irregular* cell growth do you mean something like a *cancerous* growth?" Lisa replied there was no way she could say for certain. She suggested we make a trip to a vet as soon as possible to acquire a formal medical diagnosis. Since I had come to trust her judgment implicitly, I put Codi in the car and drove the short drive to the nearest veterinarian's office offering walk-in services, instead of driving over 30 miles to see our usual vet.

From the moment I heard Lisa's words, it was clear this would be a major test of my ability to apply a spiritual approach to this situation. My mind started racing with all sorts of thoughts, most of them based in fear and worry. As I drove the short trip to the local vet, Codi stood in her usual spot on the front passenger seat staring intently out the front window. As was customary with our car trips I commanded her to *sit down* a few times. Each time she looked at me and totally ignored the instruction.

It wasn't that she didn't understand the command. No, not at all – she fully understood but defiantly did what she wanted to do anyway. That was our Codi all right, an independent spirit who was, in reality, the alpha dog of the household. Over the years we lived with her, my wife, Andrea, and I remarked many times how lucky we felt that

Codi allowed *us* to live in the house with her.

When we arrived at the vet's office and finished the registration process, it wasn't long before we were escorted into an examining room. There a vet technician weighed Codi, and also made notes regarding the reason for our visit. A few minutes later, a young and very compassionate vet named Sandra entered and asked me a series of questions. After several minutes of discussion, she recommended an x-ray and full blood workup, including a liver panel, be completed. Naturally, I agreed, and Codi soon was led away for her x-ray and blood draw. A short time later she was brought back to the room, and not long afterwards Sandra returned with the completed x-ray. At this point my heart was pumping fast as my body filled with adrenaline. I was hoping against hope Lisa was incorrect in her observation.

Referring to the x-ray, Sandra pointed out some dark shading that indicated irregular tissue on the liver. She cautioned the only way to be certain as to its nature would be to perform an ultrasound test. I then asked her what area of the organ she was referring to, thinking back to Lisa's original impression. Sandra replied that the suspect tissue was on the left lobe of the liver, very near to the rib cage; *precisely where Lisa had said it was.* 'A simply amazing effort on Lisa's part,' I briefly thought, but the fact was we still didn't know the exact nature of the problem. According to the vet, it was at least possible the tissue in question wasn't malignant, which gave me some faint amount of hope. When the results of the blood work were available the next morning we would have a much better idea of the liver's overall health, but that information alone wouldn't be enough to provide an exact diagnosis. For that, the ultra-sound obviously had to be completed.

Given Codi's importance to our family, there was no alternative but to agree to the test. It would be conducted the following afternoon at a sister facility located about 15 miles away. I also was told to phone in around 10 the next morning for the blood test results, which would likewise be faxed to the other facility. Standing there in the examining room with Sandra, the seriousness of the situation finally hit me and I was moved to tears as I shared with her how much Codi had meant to us over the years. She did her best to reassure me, cautioning it was simply too early in the process to draw any definitive conclusions about the condition. Despite those assurances, feelings of fear and sadness gripped me while considering the possibility Codi might indeed be seriously ill. After a couple more minutes of conversation, Sandra said goodbye and wished us well. We then left the examining room and prepared to leave.

After settling up at the desk we headed back to the car. As I sat down in the driver's seat I looked over at Codi, embraced her and began to cry. She quickly wiggled out of my grasp and in typical Codi style looked at me intently as if to say, "Take me home, I have work to do." I wasn't offended because being standoffish was just part of her nature, as was the fixation on *work* I referenced earlier. During the short drive home, my mind continued to focus on reviewing potential outcomes of this situation while Codi once again stood up in the passenger seat gazing out at life, clearly unaffected by what had just transpired.

When we got back home she jumped out of the car, picked up one of her Frisbees and went directly to the back door of the garage, demanding to go out and play. Andrea then came out of the house with our other dog, Heidi, who barked like crazy to greet us both and joined her pal in wanting to play. A rescue dog, Heidi joined our family a day after Christmas of 1995 as a present from my well-meaning brother Mike and his wife Roseann. As we headed out to the backyard, I began updating Andrea on what we had learned in our visit to the vet. Her eyes promptly filled with tears, triggering mine to once again do the same. We embraced for a few moments and then began tossing toys for the dogs.

Throughout the rest of that evening we made a concerted effort not to dwell on the "what ifs" of the situation, but there was no denying our deep concern about what the next day's news would bring.

2. *April 13, 2004 – Morning*

Andrea and I both awoke fairly early after a less than restful sleep. We then waited anxiously until mid-morning to call the vet's office to learn the blood test results. When I finally picked up the phone and dialed the number I was filled with dread, yet tried my best to remain hopeful. Unfortunately, whatever optimism I had quickly dimmed when a vet technician informed me the test unmistakably showed all of Codi's liver enzymes were elevated well above the norms. This suggested the presence of some type of liver disease. In spite of this news, I was cautioned once again not to jump to conclusions without seeing the results of the ultrasound test, scheduled for 11:45 a.m. that same day.

As I left the phone, Andrea clearly knew by the look on my face the news wasn't positive. Just then I felt such a deep level of sorrow that words cannot adequately describe. My thoughts of despair, however, quickly changed to expressions of anger, like 'How could this happen to *my* BC?' and 'Why Codi, she's only 12 and she has the energy of a four-year-old?' and 'This is just not fair, we always gave her the best food and medical care.' It was like I was riding an emotional seesaw with each side being a different type of *negative* emotion.

Although she was visibly upset herself, Andrea served as the steadying influence that morning by immediately admonishing me to settle down. The truth is her strength and sensibility has always been of incredible value to me, especially whenever I've been faced with emotionally challenging circumstances. She quickly reiterated the importance of not coming to conclusions until we had all of the facts. 'Easier said than done,' I thought, but I had no other reasonable choice but to agree with her, since the other option was to remain in a state of emotional distress.

Just after eleven, Codi and I left for the animal hospital where the ultrasound test would be performed. We arrived about 10 minutes early, in plenty of time to fill out the required forms. I was informed we would be seeing a vet by the name of "Dr. Tom," because he was the resident expert in this type of testing. Within a short time we were escorted into an examining room and the doctor joined us a few minutes later. As he entered the room and introduced himself, he simultaneously bent down and greeted Codi as well. My immediate feeling about him was very positive. What would ultimately transpire during the rest of the appointment would confirm that initial reaction.

Dr. Tom began by asking a series of questions to better understand Codi's condition Even though he had already reviewed the blood test results, he also took a few minutes to complete a standard health exam (i.e., eyes, ears, nose, etc.). Once that was complete, he proceeded to fill me in on details regarding the ultrasound test. He then asked if I had any questions. As I recall, I asked a number of them, my primary intent being to learn something that would give me any reason at all for optimism. Like the vet on the previous day, he emphasized the need to simply be patient, as the ultrasound test would indeed tell us all we needed to know. He then requested I retire to the lobby area to wait for the testing to be finished. Before he led Codi out of the examining room, I bent down and kissed her on the snout, and as a matter of habit reminded her to be a good girl.

While I sat reading in the waiting area, I found myself unable to concentrate for more than a couple of minutes at a time. I kept impatiently looking up at the clock every couple of minutes. After nearly an hour and half, the testing was finally completed and I was directed to a different examining room where Dr. Tom was already waiting for me. Upon entering, I noticed immediately Codi was nowhere in sight and, in that moment, a rush of concern came over me. I promptly asked where she was, and felt relieved to hear she was fine and would be brought in shortly. This feeling of relief was very short-lived; however, as Dr. Tom looked me straight in the eye and said, "Mr. Maziarek, I'm afraid I have some very bad news for you."

Once I heard those words I felt a jolt of sheer terror rip through me, followed immediately by a rapidly pounding heartbeat and tears welling up in my eyes. It took a moment for me to compose myself, at which time I asked him to continue. Taking Codi's chart and opening it on the examining table, Dr. Tom beckoned me closer to look at the printout of the ultrasound results. The bad news was the existence of patches of dark spots on the left side of the liver that had the characteristics of a particular type of cancer. Based upon the number of spots, the disease was fairly well progressed. When I asked about the possibility of a surgical solution, he indicated this was not an alternative because the growth wasn't concentrated in a single tumor.

Almost frantic, I then inquired if there was anything at all that could be done medically to deal with this type of cancer. Dr. Tom stated it was possible a chemotherapy protocol could serve to extend her life somewhat, but the drawback would be the possibility of numerous side effects that could severely curtail her quality of life. I made a remark that this was obviously a *terminal* condition, and he nodded in agreement. I then asked about how long she could be expected to live. He stated there was no way of knowing for certain, but the odds were she'd be very lucky if she made it through the rest of the year.

Although somewhat shocked by his response, I took a deep breath to calm myself and asked an additional question regarding the type of signs we should be looking for with respect to the progression of the disease. I was informed the signs of complete liver failure would include an inability to digest food properly, coupled with a complete loss of appetite and ultimately weakness to the point of exhaustion. He also stated that although she might pass on her own, the greater likelihood was at some point I'd have to make a decision to help her do so. Having been through the process of putting a dog *to sleep* one other time, I shuddered at the thought of having to experience that with Codi.

In that moment the door opened and a vet technician brought Codi into the room. She came over with her tail wagging and greeted us both, then stared directly at me with a look that seemed to say, "Dad, I'm ready to get out of this place." As I stared down at her I momentarily felt like this was all just a very bad dream, because other than looking a bit thin she appeared to be just fine. I turned to the vet once again and thanked him sincerely for all the compassion he showed. I could tell from the look in his eyes that he, too, was very saddened by the results of the test. He then escorted us out of the room and towards the front desk, shook my hand and expressed his regret for having to be the one to bring me this horrible news. I thanked him a final time, and, after we both said our goodbyes, he bent down to scratch Codi on the head, then turned and walked away.

I stood there at the front desk almost in a trance until the desk clerk brought me the credit card slip to sign. Looking back, I suppose I was in kind of a state of shock. I felt a bit numb and detached. The thought, 'This can't be happening,' kept repeating in my mind, along with 'There has to be something that can be done about this.' As the clerk handed me the receipt she asked if I would like to schedule a follow-up appointment. My response was, "No, that won't be necessary. Unfortunately, my best friend here was just diagnosed with terminal cancer."

While there was no reason to share that information with a total stranger, I guess I just felt the desire for some kind of sympathy. She immediately smiled at me and very sincerely said how sorry she was for us both. By the pained look on her face, it was obvious she loved animals and, in the course of her work, had probably heard similar words on numerous occasions. I thanked her for her understanding, and then headed out the door with Codi in tow.

3. Returning Home – April 13, 2004

As we left the vet's office I noticed immediately how wonderful it felt to get some fresh air again. The temperature was pretty warm for the middle of April and the sun was shining brightly. If this were a normal day, I'd be itching to get home and get outside with both of the dogs. However, based on what I just learned, this day was by no means ordinary. To say I was feeling despondent at that moment would be a major understatement. I truly felt lost. Despite having written a book about spirituality, a subject that emphasized the importance of not focusing on negative thoughts or emotions, the reality was that generating hope at a time when someone I loved was just pronounced terminally ill was clearly beyond me.

Once in the car, I realized I had forgotten to phone Andrea about the bad news, but when I looked for the cell phone it wasn't in its usual place in the console. 'Just as well,' I thought, because that type of information really needed to be shared in person. As I left the parking lot to head home, the thought occurred to me to stop by my brother Mike's house since it was on the way. I suppose what motivated me to follow through on that idea was a desire for some immediate emotional comfort after hearing such horrible news. The night before I had mentioned I was going to be in the area and, since my brother worked out of his house, I figured there was a good chance he'd be home. If not, perhaps his wife Roseann would be there.

It took less than 10 minutes to reach their house, and upon arriving I noticed Mike's car wasn't in the driveway.

Regardless, I left Codi in the car with the window cracked open a bit, went up to the door and rang the bell. My sister-in-law quickly answered. She excitedly stated that she was hoping I would stop by after the appointment, as she had been thinking about the two of us all day. She then asked about the results of the test and, almost as a reflex I reached out my arms, embraced her and blurted out, "Roseann, my baby has cancer on her liver and there's nothing they can do to help her." As soon as those words left my lips I started sobbing like a little boy.

She held on tightly, patting me several times on the back in an effort to comfort me. Roseann soon began crying as well, then stated again and again how deeply sorry she was. The sincerity of her sentiments in that moment was obvious and her support was tremendously important to me. She truly could relate to what I was feeling because in the past she and Mike had faced similar situations with dogs of their own. She also knew just how much Codi meant to me over the years. As we separated from the embrace, she looked out her front door and noticed Codi sitting in the front seat of the car. We then walked outside together and I headed over to the passenger side to let her out to say hello.

The BC leapt out of the car with her tail wagging and her ears back to greet Roseann. She bent down to pet her, and Codi gave her a few seconds of attention before she began her customary search of the entire yard for a tennis ball or other toy. It wasn't that she was unfriendly; it just wasn't a priority for her. Her focus in life was her work, and dealing with people always took a backseat to it. While over the years Andrea and I had become accustomed to this particular character trait, occasionally some folks we knew would lament the fact she was not a very affectionate dog. Roseann was not among that group. Instead, she chose to accept Codi exactly as she was without complaint.

After failing to find anything to play with, Codi returned from the backyard and stared up at me with a look of frustration I had seen countless times in the past. That was my cue to either get her a toy or put her back in the car to head home. Since Andrea was waiting with great anticipation to learn how things went at the vet, I felt it was best that we start back right away. I hugged Roseann again and thanked her for her kindness and support. She wished me well and then gave Codi a big hug and kissed her goodbye on the snout.

As I drove away it occurred to me that this visit was one that would forever change the way I looked at my sister-in-law. You see, in the 30-plus years I had known her we had, at best, a cordial relationship, and I must admit the primary responsibility for that was mine. I suppose a key reason for it was my assumption that we had very little in common. In any event, it was now very clear to me that all the time we knew each other we did indeed share one very important piece of common ground – a deep and abiding love of animals, particularly dogs. Looking back, this was the first of many important realizations I'd have as a result of Codi's illness.

On the way home the BC was a bit fidgety, and also continued to maintain her unwillingness to sit down during the entire drive. Based on the news we received at the vet's office a short time earlier, however, there was obviously no reason for me to try and compel her to do so. Once we got within about a mile of the house I could see she already knew we were almost home because her tail began wagging rapidly. Many might say it's ridiculous to think an animal has the level of awareness necessary to actually discern the location of its home while driving in a car. Animal or not, for whatever reason dogs do seem to intuitively *know* a lot of things they're not supposed to know based on their so-called *limited* thinking ability. If you have a dog now, or have had one in the past, I'd be surprised if your pet hasn't exhibited similar innate capabilities.

As soon as we pulled into the driveway and the garage door opened, Codi began whining to get out of the car in order to get to her critically important work of playing Frisbee. Andrea and Heidi promptly came outside to greet us both. Andrea grumbled that it was about time we got home, as she had been worried sick since we left. I apologized, but also let her know I had inadvertently forgotten the cell phone. I also told her that after leaving the vet's office I decided it would be best for us to discuss the results when I got home. In that moment the look on her face changed to one of obvious concern, and she immediately inquired as to the specifics of what the vet had found.

Before I could answer, we were interrupted by loud barking from both dogs. It was quite clear we needed to let them out the back door of the garage before it would be possible to have any sort of meaningful conversation. So, amidst the noise I walked towards the door, grabbed the dogs' toys, and all of us went outside. After we took a seat on our deck, I let Andrea know the ultrasound confirmed the BC had cancer all over the left side of her liver and there wasn't a damned thing medically that could be done about it. As I finished the last few words, my voice quivered with anger and tears once again filled my eyes. For a moment, Andrea sat there simply stunned by what I had just told her. Then she began to cry as well.

"What do you mean there's nothing they can do about it?" she sobbed. "I can't believe with all the advances in technology they are still unable to do anything at all for her." I explained that this type of cancer was not in the form of a single tumor, but was, instead, like a series of little islands of small growths, and this precluded the use of any surgical procedure. I went on to say we could choose to pursue a series of chemotherapy treatments, but there was no assurance it would have any positive effect on extending her life. And, they could wind up making her even sicker and sapping her of whatever energy she has left. I added that I couldn't imagine putting Codi through that because, if she couldn't do her work anymore, she'd just be miserable. That would certainly be no way for her to live out the rest of her days. Andrea completely agreed, then reached over and held on to me tightly for a few moments, during which time both of us began to cry again. That embrace was quickly interrupted by Codi dropping her Frisbee right at my feet, which over the years had become a very common occurrence.

We sat on the deck for a few more minutes, taking turns throwing the Frisbee for Codi and the tennis ball for Heidi. Separating the toys was something we came up with soon after Heidi arrived to make sure they wouldn't get into conflicts by vying for one or the other. The BC made some incredible catches, something that had also become customary for her over the years. Andrea then headed back into the house with both dogs to get them some water and food and to begin preparing dinner for us, in spite of the fact neither of us had much of an appetite that evening. As I looked out on the backyard and leaned back on the glider for a brief few moments, it felt like I was in a daze.

I might have continued staring out into the yard indefinitely but for the sound of some sudden barking on the part of Heidi that startled me. The fact that Codi wasn't yelping as well assured me there was nothing to be concerned about. Throughout her entire life she was very discriminating about using her voice. She would never waste her energy barking without good reason. It was as if she actually evaluated the risk and then made a conscious decision whether to react or not. For example, you'd never find her barking at a UPS truck or another dog. Other than barking to request some playtime or to demand her toy be tossed, it was usually only the sound of the doorbell or a loud knock that would compel her to make any sound at all.

Walking into the kitchen I was greeted by both dogs and Codi promptly looked at me with her standard intense stare, indicating that in her mind it was once again time to play. Just then I was struck by the difference in the way she was feeling compared to me. Clearly, my human intelligence and awareness were a disadvantage, for while I was focusing on the horrible diagnosis, she was oblivious to it. It was simply life as usual. The only time that mattered was *now.* As I pondered on that, I thought of how freeing it would be for human beings to be able to feel the same way. Unfortunately, no matter how much I tried to change my mood, I couldn't get beyond that profound feeling of sadness I felt from the moment Dr. Tom told me the news.

As the evening wore on, my mind was again besieged by a parade of angry thoughts and feelings of self-pity as well. The negative mind chatter was so relentless it was incredible. No matter what I did in an effort to distract myself it was no use. Every time I looked at Codi the same *tapes* would begin running through my mind again.

My only hope was the prospect of getting some peace by falling asleep. Unfortunately, that was not to be. As my head hit the pillow that night, I quickly dozed off, but within just a few minutes I was wide awake and my thoughts were stirring again. The difference at this point was that they weren't focused on the bad news of the day. Instead, I found myself reminiscing about how Codi first became a part of our family.

4. Border Collie Dreaming – December 1991

One Sunday morning during December of 1991, I was lounging around, reading the *Chicago Sun-Times*. I came across an article about some recently completed research into the intelligence levels of various dog breeds. This wasn't long after Andrea and I had gotten married, and we had recently discussed the idea of adding a dog to the family. The newspaper piece went into some detail describing the methodology of the testing and closed with final rankings, listing the top breed as the Scottish Border Collie, a variety I had never actually heard of previously. The article also included a picture of one of these dogs jumping high to catch a Frisbee, which, in retrospect, I suppose fascinated the little boy in me. Since my tendency was to be a very cerebral yet also athletic person, the idea of having a dog that was really bright and agile as well was very appealing.

With that seed of desire firmly planted, it didn't take very long for me to begin seeing signs reminding me about it. For example, just a few days later I was in my car driving home and noticed a woman walking a Border Collie down the street. In the past I might not have paid attention, but for some reason I looked closely and noticed the dog's characteristic black and white markings, most notably the white tip on the tail. Not long afterwards I was flipping TV channels and came across a herding competition with a single Border Collie rounding up 20 sheep and directing them into a small pen. I was mesmerized by how the dog was so methodical and focused in its work, also amazed this relatively small canine could control so many animals despite being significantly outnumbered and out-weighed. As I continued to watch the show I came to learn the dog was working only on the basis of whistle com-mands, which made the performance even more astound-ing. At that point I just knew I had to have one of those dogs someday.

Interestingly, at about the same period of time I began reading a book called "*Creative Visualization*" by Shakti Gawain. Its basic message was that all human beings have the innate ability to create what they desire in life through the conscious use of their own imagination. While reading the book, it occurred to me a great test of its claims would be to apply the principles of visualization to my desire to have a Border Collie. So, for a period of several months just about each night prior to falling asleep I spent a few minutes picturing myself in the backyard, throwing a Frisbee for a black and white dog. I combined this *imagining* work with the practical work of regularly checking the paper for ads from breeders, and stopping by the local humane society on a bimonthly basis to see if by some odd chance they had taken in a mature Border Collie or, ideally, some puppies.

At one point during the spring of 1992, Andrea and I actually went to visit a breeder about 25 miles west of our home. However, after meeting her and spending some time with a couple of her younger dogs, for whatever reason I just didn't feel drawn to them. Not long afterwards, during one of my habitual visits to the local shelter, I found they had a litter of five puppies that were of a mixed Border Collie heritage, and which had color markings suggesting they were perhaps more of that breed than anything else. Since I felt one of these pups could indeed be the right one for us, I quickly returned home to collect Andrea in the hope we could get back there before closing time to possibly select one of them.

Unfortunately, when I arrived home I picked up a phone message from her letting me know she would be arriving on a later train than usual. That meant we wouldn't be able to get to the shelter until the next evening. Given that puppies were always quick to be adopted, the obvious risk was there wouldn't be any pups left by the time we finally got there. Regrettably, that is precisely what happened and I wound up feeling somewhat disappointed of course. Nonetheless, my spiritual study to that point had taught me to remember there was always a deeper reason for things not quite working out the way I had expected.

When June of that year arrived we still hadn't found *our* puppy or perhaps, as I've come to believe over the years, the puppy had yet to find *us*. About the middle of that month, however, all that would change thanks to a series of events that we simply couldn't have predicted.

5. *Border Collie Owning –*
June 1992

It began with our decision to attend the wedding of one
of Andrea's cousins, which was to be held in Galesburg,
Illinois, about 190 miles southwest of our home. That town
also was where both of her grandmothers lived at the time.
After arriving and settling into our motel, we went to see
her paternal grandma, Marian, and her husband, Grandpa
Harley. I always enjoyed spending time with them because
they were very hospitable and down-to-earth people.

While we sat and chatted around the kitchen table, I
raised the subject of wanting a Border Collie and Marian
mentioned she recalled hearing about a nearby breeder who
had been in the business for quite some time. Unfortunately, she couldn't remember the name. She and Harley
then walked out into the backyard to do some watering
with Andrea joining them. I remained in the kitchen
to grab a drink from the refrigerator and just *happened*
to notice a copy of the *Peoria Journal Star* on one of the
kitchen chairs.

Just out of curiosity I opened the classified section to
see if by chance it had any ads for BCs. In my first scan of
the page nothing popped out, but upon closer inspection a
tiny listing caught my eyes:

> Border Collies, AIBC Registered,
> $150.00; 3 males, 2 females

The ad also included a phone number but said nothing about where the seller was located. I promptly ran

outside to tell Andrea and her grandparents about it and to ask if I could use the phone. My excitement was very obvious to all of them and, upon hearing the news, Andrea was eager to learn more about these pups as well. I headed back in the house to make the call.

The phone rang several times without an answer but eventually an older woman picked up. After exchanging greetings I asked her about the pups being advertised. She replied there was only one left, a female, but someone had already expressed interest in her. I recall being quite disappointed with the news, and apparently that emotion was evident by the change in my voice tone when I told her that I understood.

At that point I assumed the conversation was over, but she surprised me by letting me know the person who expressed interest in that pup hadn't actually committed to buying it, so she'd be happy to sell it to us instead. My mood improved immediately and I proceeded to ask her several questions about the puppy (e.g., how old she was, the color of her coat and eyes, how much she weighed). After getting answers to my questions, I decided to go ahead and commit to the purchase, but only if I could have a few moments to run it past Andrea and obtain her blessing. I quickly put the phone down and ran outside to let her know what was going on. After a brief conversation we both decided it was a good idea, and I returned to the phone to finalize the deal.

It was then the subject of the price came up, which to my delight she decided to reduce to $100.00, but only if we could pay her in cash. I eventually came to learn the primary reason for the discount was because this pup was not only the final dog in the litter, but was also the last Border Collie puppy she would ever breed since she and her husband had sold the farm and were retiring to a nearby town. I then proceeded to request directions, as in all the excitement I had failed to even think about asking where she lived. It turned out the home was located pretty far out in the country near a town called Roanoke, Illinois, somewhere northeast of Peoria.

After perhaps two minutes of writing down directions, I promised we'd pick up the pup during the afternoon of the next day. Even though she didn't seem to have any problem with that, before hanging up I felt compelled to assure her we would indeed show up. I'll always remember her reply, which in essence was, "Of course you'll come; you just don't sound like the lying type." Coming from a major city where trust on the part of either sellers or buyers wasn't very common, it really was refreshing to hear such a response. In some sense it endeared me to her and likewise reaffirmed my basic instinct to trust human nature.

Once I left the phone, I rushed outside to tell Andrea and her grandparents the good news. As we talked about it we were both very excited at the prospect of adding a new member to our family. A few minutes later we said our goodbyes to Granny and Gramps and left for the wedding. We also assured them we'd come by for an early lunch the next day prior to heading home.

The next morning we awoke with great anticipation to get on the road and pick up the new puppy. As I reflect back on the experience, I find it interesting that neither of us ever stopped to consider that we might not even like the pup's appearance and demeanor. I suppose we just instinctively *knew* this was the right thing for us to do. As promised, we stopped for a bite to eat with her grandparents as well as some additional visiting of course. During the course of the conversation, I suddenly realized we needed cash to pay for the pup, and it's a good thing I did since we were short about $70.00, and neither of us brought an ATM card or a checkbook on the trip. Fortunately Granny came to the rescue by offering to front us the cash. Over the years we frequently reminded her of how grateful we were for the critical role she played in the pup becoming a part of our family.

Completing our goodbyes we headed out to the interstate that would take us east towards Peoria. While that portion of the journey was a snap, once we exited at Highway 116N things became quite a bit more complicated. After driving perhaps 10–15 miles north we found ourselves surrounded by cornfields bounded by roads identified not by name, but by cryptic numbers. The bottom line was we were lost, and wound up driving around in circles for an hour or so. Since we didn't have a mobile phone at that time and a pay phone wasn't anywhere in sight, there wasn't any way we could call the breeder to let her know we were on the way. Just when it appeared we would never find the house we saw an old man in a dusty pickup truck approaching and flagged him down; luckily, he knew exactly where the family lived. Amazingly, we had driven past the entrance to their property a number of times but hadn't seen the small address marker partially hidden by some corn stalks.

We promptly adjusted our course and soon headed up the very long driveway towards the house, which was a nice brick ranch surrounded by expansive planted fields and some very large evergreen trees. We knocked on the door and were quickly greeted by an elderly woman with a big, bright welcoming smile on her face. After the customary introductions and a bit of a discussion about how challenging it was to find the place, she requested we follow her to the backyard so we could have our first look at the puppy.

As we left the house, we immediately noticed a small fenced-in area with a lone black and white, roly-poly puppy inside it – *the moment of truth had finally arrived.* I was filled with a feeling of excitement and anticipation, and yet at the same time I found myself feeling sad the poor little thing was all alone. That feeling faded quickly, however, as we approached and saw her balancing herself on her rear legs while clinging to the top of the fence and vigorously wagging her tail. She was simply beautiful in every respect. Although her coat was primarily black, she had distinctive white markings on her chest, her forehead, and on all four of her legs. She also had piercing eyes and an adorable little pink belly with small black spots. As Andrea and I bent down to greet her, the strength of the connection was obvious to all three of us.

The breeder could easily see this sale was complete, so she gently picked up the pup and asked us to join her back inside the house to finalize the deal with one final immunization and the delivery of a pedigree chart. As she took care of this in the kitchen we couldn't help but notice that the pup appeared to be turning her head, as if trying to listen to every word being said. We came to learn this behavior is actually characteristic of Border Collies, as these dogs are so intelligent and focused they make every effort to understand (in their own terms) everything that is occurring around them. Over the course of our life with her we would see this same behavior, literally on a daily basis. Thinking back, I suppose this endeared her to me even more, because of my own penchant for carefully analyzing life on a moment-to-moment basis. Even as I write this some fourteen years later, I can recall clearly the look on the pup's face as we prepared to leave that day. If she could talk, I got the feeling she would have said something like, "It's about time you got here."

We had prepared for the 150-mile ride home with the new *baby* by getting a small box at a Galesburg grocery store, then lining it with newspaper and one of Granny's old towels. Our plan was to have the pup stay in the backseat. However, it quickly became abundantly clear by her whining that she had an entirely different idea in mind. After just a couple of minutes driving with that racket, Andrea reached back into the box, lifted the puppy and towel out and placed them both on her lap. Amazingly, all the fussing and fidgeting stopped in just a few seconds and then perhaps a minute later she was sound asleep. Looking over at the two of them really was a touching sight, as the tiny black and white pup had quite obviously taken to her new *mommy*, and the look on Andrea's face was one of complete love and contentment. The image of them bonding in this manner served to reinforce my confidence that we had indeed made the right decision.

For the next hour or so, the pup remained in this peaceful state and only awoke when we stopped at a Wendy's to use the restroom and to give her a potty break as well. Once back on the road, she promptly went back to sleep on Andrea's lap. It was about this time it dawned on us that we had yet to give a name to the little one. This became our focus during the next hour or so, and, as I recall, we considered lots of alternatives. We wanted to avoid ultra-common names, and yet desired some moniker that would be easy to say and have a nice ring to it. This truly became a collaborative effort and, though I'm not sure exactly how it came about, we eventually happened upon the name Cody, but with a bit of a twist, in that we chose to spell it *Codi* instead to better reflect her femininity. With that big step out of the way, it wasn't much longer until we arrived home as a family for the first time.

That first night we spent a lot of time playing and frolicking with her, laying the groundwork for what would become one of the most important relationships in our lives. Even at just ten weeks of age she was already showing obvious signs of a level of focus that would become one of her trademarks over the years. We also took several photos that evening, including the first two shown later in the photo gallery. As the evening came to a close, the stark realization came to us that neither of us had ever actually trained a puppy before. In the past that had been the responsibility of one or both of our parents. One thing was certain; we were clearly in for some interesting lessons over the next several weeks.

6. Border Collie Parenthood and Training – Summer 1992

As bedtime arrived that first night of our canine parent-hood, we faced the challenge of what to do with our new family member while we slept. Per the breeder's instructions I had prepared a dog crate, and now it was time to use it. The truth was neither of us really wanted to put Codi in there for the night, but all we'd read and heard said it was the best thing to do. According to the experts, she would consider it a *den* and make herself comfortable curling up with the blanket we provided. And, a ticking alarm clock we planned to put in there hopefully would remind her of her mother's heartbeat.

'Solid theory,' we thought, 'but how would it work in practice?' With midnight about to strike, it obviously was time to find out. The pup was already dozing on the living room floor, so surely it wouldn't be a problem to simply shift her to the crate, which we had placed in the kitchen. So, I gently picked her up and placed her inside, closed the door, shut off the light, and walked toward the bedroom where Andrea was waiting for me.

Within seconds of my getting into bed, it was evident the crating approach was not working quite as the experts said it would. Based on the high-pitched whining that had begun, Codi was *not* going for it at all. Turning on the light I looked at Andrea and said, "Now what?" Half asleep, she looked up and quickly admonished me to stick with the plan because it was the only sensible approach. Even though she was right (as she usually is) I couldn't stand listening to the crying, so I headed back into the kitchen to see if I could do something to quiet her down.

As soon as I flicked the light on, the whining stopped and was replaced by the thumping of her little tail against the side of the crate. I opened the door, picked her up, and held her to my chest with one arm while stroking her with my other hand. I sat down on the couch and started talking to her as if she was a little kid. While I don't remember the exact words, in essence I reassured her as best as I could and waited for her to fall asleep again. As soon as she did I put her back in the crate and went back to the bedroom.

Once again, shortly after climbing into bed the crying resumed. Andrea, who was immediately stirred from sleep, told me again to *stick with the plan*. I remember saying to her that the crying was just too difficult to handle. In response she told me to close the bedroom door. While I hated to leave the poor little pup alone, at the time I knew it was best so I shut the door, put in earplugs and went to sleep.

Codi eventually adapted to the crate, but it would be inaccurate to imply that she actually ever liked being inside it. In some sense, I feel she merely tolerated our use of it despite her knowing that it really wasn't even necessary.

The days and weeks that followed were filled with lots of bonding and many hours of training, including several sessions with a Border Collie trainer referred to us by a friend. Codi's progress was swift and steady, as it took just a couple of weeks for her to be fully house-trained. It didn't take long for the crate to be returned to the basement and for her to be given free reign of the house, even when we left for short periods of time.

Within three weeks, she had easily picked up basic commands (e.g., sit, stay, lay down) and had learned to ask to go outside. All of this reinforced what I had originally read about Border Collies regarding their intelligence and trainability. She was, indeed, incredibly smart and focused and she clearly demonstrated this when it came to what quickly became her life's mission – to *work* as a Frisbee dog. An experienced dog breeder we knew referred to this behavior as a *toy obsession*, which in reality was a very fitting term.

It's my belief that the source of Codi's fixation was actually an ingrained instinct of the breed to herd out of loyalty, love, and respect for their handlers. In Codi's case, the Frisbee (or, at times, other toys) replaced sheep or other type of livestock as the object of attention, and she not only chased it for fun, but also because she literally felt it was her *mission* to do so. In any event, this obsession ensured she could be easily managed, as the toy itself could effectively be used as a reward for good behavior or to inspire her to take some desired action.

Just about every dog lover thinks his or her pet is really smart in some respect, so it wouldn't surprise you to know I just marveled at Codi's learning ability. Whether she was more intelligent than other dogs didn't matter to me. I was simply very grateful to have a canine companion with that level of focus. Truth is, she reminded me of my own intensity when it came to work, something which served to further strengthen our bond. What was particularly beneficial that summer of '92 was the fact I had plenty of time to work with her. This was because of my involvement in a high tech startup company, which, at that point, didn't require much of my efforts on the marketing front. So, we essentially spent all of our days together playing, walking, and training.

With her basic instruction complete by mid-summer, there was one last critical lesson she needed to be taught – how to respect the boundaries of the yard. Since there wasn't a fence in the front of the house, it was vital she learn to remain on the property at *all* times. I knew this was possible because I had seen my mother train two other dogs to do so. I was therefore confident Codi could pick it up as well.

The approach is to use a choke collar and leash, and then allow the dog to walk freely toward the street or other boundary. The moment the border it is reached, a firm tug on the leash and a stern *No* is applied. The trick of course is for the dog to come to respect the boundary without the leash, and even without the need to say no. To ensure she really got the lesson, I decided to add another element to the teaching, the acid test of respecting the boundary while chasing a Frisbee or a ball.

After perhaps eight repetitions of the basic lesson off-leash, it was time for this big test. I then deliberately threw her prized Frisbee into the street, she took off after it at full-speed, and at the precise moment she reached the curbside I screamed "*NO!*" She stopped immediately and the toy skipped across the asphalt. She then took a few steps back and turned to look at me for her next direction. I was absolutely amazed she got it the first time. By the fifth repetition she was stopping curbside even without the "no" command. From that day forward, Codi never once left the yard, no matter what the temptation was. She could, therefore, be trusted on her own outside. This saved us from having to put her on a leash and face the elements whenever she needed to go out. With a dog like that it's very easy to get spoiled.

By August of that first summer, Codi was just four months old yet fully trained in basic obedience. My focus with her then shifted to further developing her Frisbee skills. Since she was already obsessed with it, the effort necessary to make her really proficient wasn't very significant. She so loved playing with the Frisbee, that as soon as I would pull it out of her toy box, she was completely riveted upon it.

We always played in the backyard, where there was ample space for her to run. Initially, we worked on the basic 'toss and catch' approach with me learning to throw it properly and she to grab it before it hit the ground. After numerous repetitions over several weeks, we both improved tremendously. It brought me great joy to watch her work, and in some sense I suppose it also helped me get in touch again with the little boy I once was. For Codi, it truly was her purpose in life. The delight in her eyes as she galloped back with it in her mouth each time was quite a sight to behold.

For example, whenever she would make a particularly stellar catch, she would approach with a look that essentially said, "I'm *bad* and I know it." Since she was so intense and interested in learning new things, I always looked for ways to capitalize upon those traits. One day, while watching her sprint out ahead of the Frisbee, I thought, 'Wow, she reminds me of a wide receiver in football.' From that thought emerged the idea to teach her to begin her sprint only *after* I spoke a specific word, much like a quarterback tells his teammates to "go on three."

So, similar to the QB I created a string of words (i.e., ready, set, hut 1, hut 2, hike) that I used precisely in order. It took perhaps six repetitions for her to learn to only proceed when the word *hike* was spoken. From that point through the rest of her life she never forgot the training, and I cannot express to you how much fun it was to run that *play* with her virtually every day.

As the summer of '92 came to a close, Andrea and I thought it would be fun to take Codi down to Lake Michigan to see how she might respond to the water. While Border Collies aren't known to be water dogs like Labs, for example, we had heard of stories of dogs in the breed's native Scotland that were known to lead an entire flock of sheep across a stream. We were curious as to whether Codi had such an orientation. Since we didn't happen to have any sheep available, we thought perhaps a tennis ball might provide comparable motivation for her to enter the lake.

Interestingly, when we tossed the ball in the water, her toy obsession compelled her to go in after it. However,

the look in her eyes on the way out clearly demonstrated
a major distaste for the experience (see the photo gallery).
Truly, the way she held on to me when I picked her up on
the beach was really dramatic. She obviously hated the
water, so we never subjected her to it again.

During September, the start-up company I was involved
with finally required more active participation on my part.
This meant I would have to spend quite a bit more time on
the phone than I had in the past. It didn't take long before
this new responsibility collided with the routine Codi and
I had established since she joined the family a few months
earlier. She had become very accustomed to letting loose
with an occasional loud bark whenever I failed to pick up
her toy or ball within a minute or so. Because she was so toy-
obsessed she couldn't help but remind me to toss it again.

While this was all well and good when it was just us
two, it certainly wouldn't be acceptable if I was doing some
business on the phone. The obvious solution would be to
put the toy away when the phone would ring. The problem
was she would occasionally bark in that manner simply to
let me know it was time to play. I wasn't exactly sure how
to address this until one day when I received a phone call
right in the middle of a play session. There wasn't time to
do anything but pick up the call, and, once I did, it was
just a matter of minutes before the first bark sounded,
quickly followed by a few more. I apologized to the caller,
put him on hold briefly, and then followed an instinct to

lightly grab Codi's snout while at the same time firmly saying the word *quiet*.

Over the next few minutes I repeated this process a number of times, requesting the caller's patience each time a bark rang out so I could repeat the command. Interestingly, Codi came up with a hybrid behavior of firmly clacking her top and bottom teeth together, but not actually making any barking sound at all. Andrea and I eventually coined the term "fake bark" to describe this rather novel behavioral adaptation, which the BC then maintained throughout the balance of her healthy life. Thanks to her flexibility, I was able to successfully conduct business without callers even knowing that I was playing with my dog at the same time. I must admit, however, there were numerous times when that teeth-clacking became pretty annoying!

Codi's speed in picking up the "fake bark" behavior convinced me this particular Border Collie was so intelligent she could potentially be trained to do all sorts of interesting things. While we probably only scratched the surface of her abilities, we did come up with some very unusual activities for her to do that first summer, and beyond.

For example, Andrea had the idea to install a small bell at the back door that Codi could then ring to let us know she needed to go outside and go potty. It took just a handful of repetitions to teach her to connect the act of sounding the bell with getting a trip outdoors, but soon

Codi figured out she could also use that bell as an excuse to get out into the yard to play Frisbee. It therefore didn't take long for us to have to remove the bell because it was being rung far too often!

Another illustration was an inspiration I had one day to teach Codi to go fetch the newspaper. I figured this would be a very valuable skill for her to have on days when we were experiencing some inclement weather. She ultimately learned the behavior in fairly short order, but we got the sense from the look in her eyes that she only did it to appease us. It was if she felt like the action was beneath her, or perhaps she was annoyed at our asking her to fetch something that clearly wasn't a toy. Either way, this was not a task that she ever took to with any sort of zeal.

She had a similar reaction one day when we spent some time teaching her to grab a TV remote control that had fallen on the floor. After about five repetitions she finally completed the act, but the growling noise she made in the process of delivering it to us indicated she was pretty aggravated about having to complete such a trivial task. We always got a similar reaction from Codi each time we asked her to do the popular *bang trick*. This is the trick where the trainer points their index finger at the dog and pretends to shoot it while saying the word "bang." In response to this command, the dog is then supposed to quickly lie down and play dead. Codi learned this trick very easily, but it was obvious from the way she literally rolled her eyes at us that she was never happy about doing it.

The Codi eye-roll was actually something we saw many times over the years, as it ultimately became one of her trademark behaviors. Whenever she'd express herself in this way, it always reminded us of the dog Gromit from the award-winning "*Wallace and Gromit*" claymation short movie features (see www.wallaceandgromit.com). The creator of those films, Nick Parks, had a unique way of making Gromit's eye-rolls incredibly expressive and realistic. If you ever had the chance to see Codi roll her eyes, I'm sure you'd agree that her resemblance to Gromit was actually quite striking!

By the time October 1992 arrived, Andrea and I had developed quite the intense bond with Codi. She had woven her way deep into our hearts and become an integral part of the very essence of our lives.

7. *Revelations – April 14, 2004*

When I awoke the day following the diagnosis, Codi was lying in her usual spot by the side of the bed giving the impression that this was just another day. After the horrible news of the previous day, I didn't feel like things could ever be even somewhat normal again. The thought of this death sentence being held over the head of my beloved BC was just too much to handle.

After saying my morning prayers I rolled out of bed and knelt down on the floor to pet Codi and also took the opportunity to whisper, "I love you," in one of her ears. I greeted Heidi in a similar way, and then headed over to the bathroom to take a shower. In some sense I was still in a state of shock as I ran the water and prepared to step into the tub. Standing there with the water streaming down my face, I started to replay the events of the previous day. A deep sadness enveloped me again, but this time it was even more intense. At one point I simply started sobbing like a little child and said aloud, "No, no, God, please don't take my baby."

In that moment I literally heard a voice in my ear, much like individuals with clairaudient skills reportedly hear, that stated very directly, *"She's not dead yet!"* It continued on, emphasizing to me I must shift my thoughts toward being totally focused in the *present*, for in that moment all was well – she was alive and we were together as always.

What an incredible revelation this was, for it shook me out of my sorrow and resignation, and likewise inspired me to make the absolute most out of every moment I had left with her. It was at that time I made a commitment to just *be* with her through whatever would ultimately unfold as a result of her illness. One of the first steps I took was to cancel a visit with a friend in Florida that was planned for the following week. Travel was clearly not an option for me, for now the focus would be totally on Codi – supporting her, caring for her, loving her. She brought me so much joy over the years, it was certainly the least I could do.

Toweling off from my shower, another thought came to me, 'Why do I have to accept this diagnosis?' As an author of a book about spiritual growth, I'd had the opportunity to meet and interact with talented healers who operated outside the world of conventional medicine. 'There is indeed a spiritual solution to every problem,' I thought, 'so why couldn't there be a miraculous healing for Codi?'

Whereas I had awakened with a feeling of despair, now I was energized with the thought that I could actually *do* something to address the problem. I simply would not take this lying down! There had to be someone in my circle of contacts who could overcome the limitations of traditional veterinary medicine and bring healing to the BC.

After having a seat in my office and turning on my computer, I began to think about this subject with a great deal of focus. The first person who came to mind was my energy healer friend, Lisa Jacobsen, for if she could identify her condition so accurately, she potentially could assist in healing Codi as well. The second individual that popped into my head was my friend, John Honey, an acupuncturist who also had an uncanny ability to sense abnormal energy patterns within his patients, and to assist them in their release. I also recalled an energy healing technique taught to me years earlier by a woman named Nicole Kubow, as it could potentially help Codi as well.

Looking down at the BC, who had stretched out behind my office chair, I smiled and actually felt optimistic for the first time since the diagnosis.

8. *Taking Action – April 15, 2004*

Except for some very obvious weight-loss indicated by her now more visible spine, Codi showed no other outward signs of a *terminal* illness. Nonetheless, the diagnosis made two days earlier was something very real and now was indeed the time for some action on my part.

My first step was to call Lisa the energy healer and ask for any assistance she might be able to provide. Earlier in her life she had overcome a very serious autoimmune disease and, in the process of her own recovery was drawn to the healing vocation. I had personally worked with her in the past, successfully resolving some physical issues I was experiencing. I had also referred a few friends to Lisa, with one woman in particular having a complete healing of some long-standing lower back pain after just one session.

Because of these experiences, I really felt Lisa could be of help to Codi in some way. With great anticipation I dialed her number and fortunately was able to reach her on the first ring. As usual, she was happy to hear from me and listened attentively as I described in detail what had occurred since her initial energy scan of the BC. She didn't appear surprised by the news at all because, at some level, I believe she knew it was cancer from the first moment she peered into Codi's energy field. It simply wasn't her responsibility to confirm the diagnosis at that time.

Once I'd filled her in on all the facts, my voice began to quiver a bit as I politely asked her if there was anything at all she could do to reverse the BC's condition. After quite a long pause her response was compassionate but direct: "Lovey, I know how much you love your friend and I would like nothing more than to tell you I could be of help to her. Unfortunately, there is nothing I can do because my healing work is focused on working with people."

In that moment, my newfound optimism was momentarily shaken. While I tried not to have any expectations of Lisa, the truth was that her response really disappointed me. Since she was a very direct person, however, I knew "no meant no" and therefore made no attempt to persuade her to change her mind. Instead, I thanked her for the time she spent with me, and then we said our goodbyes.

After leaving the phone I took a few minutes to think deeply about what I had just heard. Even though I felt somewhat down and discouraged, I wouldn't allow this setback to diminish my resolve. There was always the other option I referred to earlier, and it was time to get busy and pursue it. So, I promptly phoned my acupuncturist, Dr. John Honey, to see if he would be willing to treat a canine. He wasn't able to speak with me, so I left a message with his receptionist and then waited for him to call.

Later that day John returned my call and was very supportive. He admitted this would be the first time he'd examine a dog, and told me to bring Codi by the following Saturday after his regular office hours were over. I hung up the phone feeling optimistic once again. Like Lisa, John had some amazing healing skills, and in my view there was no reason to believe they couldn't be used to help the BC. Saturday was just two days away. I hoped the time would pass quickly.

9. A Breakthrough? – April 17, 2004

When Saturday finally arrived, I was filled with anticipation about what might transpire later in the day at Dr. Honey's office. After my morning prayer time, I knelt down on the floor to pet Codi, and to talk with her a bit about the appointment. If you currently have a dog or have had one in the past, I imagine you've done a fair share of speaking to your pet as well. Because of our emotional connection with pets, it's not much of a stretch to feel they really do understand us at some level.

In my own case, I always spoke to Codi as if she understood every single word I said. This day was no exception. I explained to her where we were going, who we were seeing, and some of the things she *might* experience (e.g., acupuncture needles). I asked her to be a good girl during whatever treatment may occur, and to be *open* to the healing work John might do. To a non-dog lover witnessing this conversation, I might be considered at best eccentric, at worst, a bit touched in the head. For me, it was only natural to speak to my best friend in this way.

Codi looked at me intently as she always did, but when I bent down further to kiss her on the snout, she pulled her head away a bit and then rose from the floor. This type of rejection was actually quite characteristic of the BC. It wasn't that she didn't love me, she was just ready to play some Frisbee (i.e., do some work!).

With a brief play session completed, it was time for some lunch followed quickly by our departure. We set off for John's office at about 11:30 for the one-hour drive.

Codi was her usual independent self in the car, refusing to sit down as her eyes constantly scanned the on-rushing scenery. When we finally arrived at our destination, she was quite anxious to leave the car and explore a bit. Once she took a bio-break, I clipped on her lead and we headed inside. John emerged from one of his examining rooms and greeted me warmly, as usual. He then smiled down at her and said, "Hi boy." The fact that Codi was a female didn't really occur to John, because to him everyone and everything is just energy in motion. Besides, he'd never really been much of a dog person anyway.

John asked if we could give him a few minutes to finish up with a patient. I, of course, nodded yes, and he then walked away. At that moment, a rather fortuitous encounter occurred with another man visiting the office. He approached us in a very friendly manner, first bending down to greet Codi and then reaching his hand out to me. Introducing himself as Tommy, he went on to state he was there to play guitar with John once he'd completed his appointments for the day.

Tommy inquired as to the purpose of our visit and I responded with a quick summary of our situation. When he heard the news about Codi's condition, his eyes showed great compassion. He went on to explain that he was a real dog lover and also told me he had previously experienced a similar situation with one of his own pups. More importantly, he took the opportunity to educate me regarding an immune system enhancement product for dogs, called Transfer Factor Canine Complete, sold by a company called 4Life Research. Normally, I'd be suspicious about

what seemed like a sales pitch, but Tommy's compassion
for Codi convinced me he was sincere. I told him I'd definitely check out the Web link and thanked him for sharing
it with me.

After a few minutes more, John reappeared and
motioned for us to step into his office. We chatted for a little
while, catching up on each other's lives since it had been
some time since we'd last seen each other. I filled him in
on the basics of the formal veterinary diagnosis and he just
smiled in response. You see, John is the type of doctor who
always holds a vision of perfect health for his patients. This is
because he knows that, at the fundamental level, any illness
is just an energy imbalance. And, since energy is impres-
sionable based on the intention of both the patient and the
physician, all disease, therefore, is theoretically curable.

This is not to suggest that healing will always result
because, quite obviously, this isn't the case in practice.
What it does mean, however, is the potential for healing
is indeed always present. In Codi's case, clearly my intention was for her to overcome this disease and, based on a
reasonable assumption that she shared this intention, it was
therefore possible that she could do so.

With the preliminaries out of the way, John stooped
down and put his hands on either side of Codi's rib
cage. He then began to slowly change the position of his
hands, ever so slightly, until he reached a point where he
paused for about a minute or so. This was the precise area
where the cancer had been found on the ultra-sound test.
Standing up, he said, "Jeff, this feels like a mass of *grief*
energy – a deep sadness, if you will."

I asked him what she could be so unhappy about in order to take this type of energy on. He explained that it wasn't really sadness in the conventional sense. Rather, Codi, as part of the animal kingdom, was playing her role in balancing the energy of the entire planet. In other words, she had taken on this grief as an element of her very nature and purpose.

If this sounds a bit too bizarre or metaphysical for you, I understand. Yet, we humans have so little knowledge of what exists in unseen dimensions that John's explanation was, in my view, certainly *possible*. Assuming he was correct, I asked how this might impact her prospects for healing. John responded that Codi had the ability to release this energy, if she so intended. To assist her in this regard, he suggested I actually tell her each day to "push this grief energy out of her liver, move it through her legs and paws, and put it down to the earth." According to John, the planet itself had the power to transform it into harmless, pure energy.

This made sense to me, based on some things I'd read about Native American beliefs about the Earth's innate energy healing capabilities. And, since Codi could not be helped by conventional veterinary medicine, it certainly *couldn't hurt* to try doing what John recommended. I then asked if he felt there was anything he could do to help her from an acupuncture perspective. He replied that he didn't feel it would benefit this condition but he did recommend some Chinese herbs for cancer support. I grabbed a couple of bottles and also inquired as to his fee for the day's services. John said, "No charge," as it was the least he could do for a good friend who'd had a very tough week. I thanked him for his kindness and headed for the exit with Codi. The long ride home gave me plenty of time to think about everything John had said. I felt more hopeful than before, because now, at least, there were a couple of things I could actually *do* to help her.

In addition to following John's suggestion, I decided that each morning I would begin using the energy clearing technique mentioned in an earlier chapter. The basic approach is to ask God for healing energy that matches the exact frequency of the energy you want removed from the subject. You then respectfully ask for that energy to attach itself to the diseased energy and travel out of the subject[3]. If this also sounds a bit "out there" to you, consider the whole process as a type of focused prayer.

My friend, Nicole, who taught me this approach, assured me that miraculous healings were known to occur for those who used it. The ultimate key to its success is a clear and focused intention on the part of the subject and the practitioner. In our case, there certainly was a strong intent on my part for this to succeed. I couldn't imagine Codi wouldn't be on the exact same page as I. 'Why wouldn't she want to be healed?' I thought.

Starting the next day we'd begin the new treatment regimen in earnest. The rest of the current day would be focused on playing and hanging out together. As I spent time with her that afternoon, I found myself recalling some of the most memorable examples of the intensity that had become one of her trademarks over the years.

10. Codi's Intensity

Earlier in the book I referred several times to Codi's uncanny ability to be singularly focused. Nowhere was this trait more evident than in her approach to playing Frisbee. There was simply nothing that could distract her gaze from that flying disk. I'll never forget two instances in particular, for they were the crowning examples of just how incredibly intense she could be.

The first of these occurred before our second dog, Heidi, joined the family. One afternoon while in the midst of a regular play session in the backyard, I noticed an opossum ambling toward us heading toward the front of the house. This was a bit of an odd sight because they tend to be nocturnal animals. Here it was broad daylight and she and Codi were about to meet. I had heard these animals *could* become dangerous if provoked, but it was too late to do anything to stop it.

During the few seconds that I evaluated the situation, I neglected to pay close attention to Codi, who was doing her customary behavior of staring at the Frisbee with the classic Border Collie *hypnotic eye*, and her head and shoulders in a lowered position. The hypnotic eye characteristic is the quality that makes BCs so superb in herding sheep, using their eyes to guide a herd without the need to nip or bark. At the exact time I looked down at the BC, the opossum came across her field of vision. Interestingly, the animal paused for a brief moment to look at Codi, who at the same time just slightly shifted her eyes to the left to briefly return the gaze, all the while maintaining her pose and fixation on the Frisbee.

Seeing there would be no need for a confrontation, the opossum headed off to continue its journey. I was truly stunned at Codi's intense focus and dedication to her work. If Heidi (a Flat Coat Retriever mix who loved to chase squirrels) was around at the time, there's little doubt some type of altercation would have occurred.

The second memorable example of Codi's intensity occurred during the midst of a heavy snowstorm we experienced one winter. This particular day I brought her into the front yard with me and began clearing the driveway of snow. Naturally, her Frisbee was part of the experience. With us both working something would have to give, because I couldn't complete my task very quickly if I was constantly bending down to pick up and toss the toy. So, Codi was left to patiently wait for a toss every few shovel loads of snow. It really was quite a sight to see, Codi staring intently at her toy in the middle of a blinding snowstorm.

As if that concentration wasn't enough, what happened at one point would put a firm exclamation point on her storied ability to focus. While she was staring intently at her Frisbee I accidentally threw an entire shovel load of snow directly on her head. What was Codi's response? Other than blinking a few times to get her vision clear, her posture never changed in any respect. She made no attempt to shake off the snow, for doing so would have broken her concentration, and left her unprepared for a toss if I so happened to pick up and throw the toy.

That was my girl, as reliable and predictable as a Swiss watch. When I related this story to Andrea she just smiled and said, "Like father like daughter." Over the many winters we spent together there were many other times I'd purposely throw a shovel full of snow on her head to test her, and the result was always the same.

While the preceding two stories are the most dramatic examples of Codi's intensity, she also demonstrated similar behavior every time she would have the opportunity to play Frisbee in front of a crowd. This became evident the first time we stopped by a local park with her. We were on our way home from an errand or two, and since we had Codi in the car we thought it would be fun to let her play in the wide-open space. Because she could be managed very easily through the use of her toy, there was no concern about her running away or bothering anybody.

On that particular day, there were a number of people walking in the park and some seated as well. After we parked and let Codi out she immediately assumed her play-ready position. I started with a few warm-up tosses, and then we got really serious. We ran a few football plays, and I also tossed a few high floaters that required her to closely follow the flight of the disk in order to estimate where it would actually land.

It took just a few minutes for her to attract a small crowd of onlookers, which included both adults and children. As the group assembled it was obvious Codi clicked up her intensity another notch or two. When she made a great catch her *swagger* upon the return trip was even more pronounced. When she failed to make the grab (usually my fault), she'd hustle back even more aggressively to return the disk for another toss. She was indeed a performer, and to her this was the main stage.

While giving such performances, her concentration also showed itself in what some spectators felt was a negative manner. It wasn't that she growled at people or threatened them in any way; she just ignored any attempt on their part to pet her. Usually it was a little kid who would approach her during one of her brief rest periods. The child would first look to us for approval to pet her, and afterwards reach down to stroke her head. In the exact moment the child's hand would move down to touch her, Codi would deliberately lower her head even further to ensure the attempt would fail.

This was actually a very comical behavior to witness, as her body language effectively said, "Leave me alone, I've got work to do." The person was typically taken aback by her response to their advance, and sometimes would ask if she was an unfriendly dog. Our response was always to politely explain that she was a working dog who just didn't want to be bothered while on the job. We also let them know she always did the same thing to us in such situations. It wasn't personal at all to Codi, it was just business.

The fact was her intensity made her appear aloof, or perhaps in some sense a bit arrogant. We just learned not to take it to heart. We knew she loved us. It just wasn't her nature to express it the way most dogs usually do. That love, however, was very evident whenever we'd return home from being out for a spell, as each time we were greeted by an aggressively wagging tail. And, sometimes, if we were very lucky, we even got a small lick on our chins!

With mature dogs it's the same as with people, for relationships to work you must learn to accept and appreciate them as they are. While Codi's intensity always provided me with great satisfaction, I'm happy to say she also had a rarely seen humorous side that was equally as endearing.

11. Codi's Comedy

Previously I mentioned that Codi would usually respond with a very comical eye-roll whenever we asked her to do something she evidently felt was beneath her. However, this wasn't her only amusing behavior. Over the years there were plenty of times when she would let her guard down and do something totally out of her typically very serious character.

Perhaps Codi's most humorous exploit was something we ultimately came to call "going Border Collie Crazy," or *BCC* for short. It all started when she was about five months old, coinciding with the time when we began to leave her alone in the house for longer periods of time. One day, upon returning from a shopping trip that kept us away for longer than we had ever been before, the BC greeted us enthusiastically at the back door and then immediately launched into a high-speed romp through the house.

This wasn't just a quick gallop from one end of the abode to the other and back again. No, this was a sustained burst of pent-up energy that included jumping on and off the couch, crawling on her belly under the cocktail table, rising up again and sprinting down the hall to the bedroom, leaping on and off the bed, circling a padded chair, then repeating the same process at least twice more until she finally got it out of her system. It essentially happened so fast that all we could do was stand back and laugh hysterically as this wild-eyed Border Collie treated our entire house like it was the setting for an agility competition!

This riotous and very entertaining behavior was actually something we had the opportunity to enjoy on many occasions over the first few years of Codi's life. She eventually stopped doing it soon after Heidi joined the family, most likely because someone was finally there to keep her company when we were away from the house. Although it's been well over a decade since Codi last went BCC, just the thought of her running insanely through the house in that manner still brings a big smile to my face.

Another of Codi's comedic antics happened out of the blue one day when she was about a year old. I was in the process of brushing my teeth while walking around the house. When I sat down on a chair in front of the TV, she suddenly leapt up next to me and starting licking the toothpaste that had leaked out of the corner of my mouth. Andrea, who also was in the room, started laughing out loud and, even though I immediately pushed the BC away, the seed was planted for a behavior that would ultimately continue for years.

Maybe it was the spearmint flavor that hooked her, or perhaps an unconscious desire to improve her dental hygiene. Whatever it was, from that day forward whenever I brushed my teeth I had to remain on guard for a potential sneak attack of toothpaste licking! Because of this, I made sure to never again sit down while brushing. But as the picture of Codi putting her paws on the bathroom sink (shown later in the photo gallery) demonstrates, that behavioral adjustment alone couldn't ensure that the BC wouldn't try an alternative way to get another taste. Over the years, the fact that I thwarted her advance every time she tried never deterred her from trying again. And, no matter how many times she did so, we always enjoyed a good giggle over it.

When playing with her Frisbee, or any other toy for that matter, Codi always came across as a very confident dog. In addition, the fact she never cowered in front of any human that approached might have led anyone who interacted with her to conclude that she was a very powerful being. The funny thing was, though, this self-assured persona didn't transfer over to the times she connected with other dogs. In fact, except for Heidi, Codi recoiled whenever another dog came close to her and, God forbid if they actually tried to sniff her behind! At such times she put on a "terrified puppy" act that left us feeling a bit embarrassed and usually led to some hearty laughter on the part of the humans who witnessed the interaction.

Although we had become accustomed to Codi's excessive shyness around other dogs, during the midst of a walk around the neighborhood one day she took this timidity to another level. Seemingly out of nowhere, a tiny Golden Labrador puppy came darting into the street to greet us. In the pup's zeal to introduce herself she just about frightened the BC half to death. In fact, Codi was so startled by this canine infant that she literally tried to jump into my arms. Andrea and I just burst out laughing at the sight of this normally intense and determined Border Collie being intimidated by such a harmless little dog barely a third of her size. Based on this experience, it was a darned good thing Codi didn't end up living on a farm because, if she had, the sheep might never have been brought in from pasture.

Codi's toy obsession wasn't limited to just Frisbees and tennis balls, as she also was fascinated with any type of dog toy, particularly those that made a squeaking sound. Each time we'd throw one for her she'd squeak the darned thing 10 or 20 times before dropping it on the floor for us to toss again. While that behavior alone was pretty humorous, what always gave us a hearty laugh was her habit of quickly bouncing her front legs up and down whenever we'd turn the table on her by squeaking the toy in rapid succession. While doing this we'd also say "dancey-dancey" to her a few times, because it literally appeared as if she were dancing in a very rhythmic motion. The truth is she was probably just so annoyed with our delay in tossing the toy that she simply had to vent her frustration in some way! Over the years I lost count of the number of toys we were forced to replace because of Codi's ability to wear out the squeaker device in them so swiftly.

As a rule, the vast majority of the people who interacted with Codi only experienced her renowned intensity as a toy-obsessed Border Collie. Other than in rare instances (like the attack of the Golden Lab puppy) it was usually just Andrea and I, or her dog-sitter Rick, who had the opportunity to see the BC's comedic side in action. One notable exception occurred once when we needed to go out of town and my sister Jan and her family volunteered to take care of Codi for a few days. Their dog, Mickey, had recently passed, so she and her daughters, Michele and Lauren, were really looking forward to having a dog around the house again.

When we dropped the BC off on a Friday afternoon, the girls showed obvious excitement at the prospects of having Codi with them for an entire weekend. They also particularly were looking forward to playing Frisbee with her. We said our goodbyes and off we went, feeling very confident that she was in great hands. After all, not only were they very responsible people, they also knew how much Codi meant to us both.

As it turned out, on the following day during a play session, one Frisbee toss Michele made accidentally floated outside of her line of sight with Codi in hot pursuit. When the BC failed to return after about a minute Michele started calling her name. After perhaps a minute more, she still neither saw nor heard any sign of Codi. It didn't take long for Michele to start to panic a bit, so she ran in the house to enlist the aid of Jan and Lauren in locating her.

The three of them then spread out and began looking all around the property, calling Codi's name the entire time. Finally, after frantically searching for a few minutes more, Michele looked behind some overgrown bushes next to the house and found Codi, stuck in one of the basement window wells with the Frisbee still in her mouth. Apparently, the BC was unwilling to drop it and, as a result, she couldn't bark and let them know her whereabouts!

Within seconds Jan and Lauren joined Michele in looking down at the BC in the window well, at which point all of them began laughing like crazy about her calm demeanor in the face of such a potentially stressful predicament. When relating these events to me, Michele remarked that the moment she came across her, the look on Codi's face seemed to say, "What the heck took you so long to find me?"

12. *The Healing Program: April 18, 2004 – July 2, 2004*

With renewed optimism based on our visit with Dr. Honey, I eagerly took on the task of helping Codi to heal her disease. Each morning she'd receive her regimen of Chinese herbs followed by an energy healing session using the technique referred to earlier in Chapter 9. Typically, the session lasted for a half-hour or more and, afterwards, I would lie down on the floor in front of her, look her right in the eyes and tell her she didn't have to keep that nasty energy in her liver.

I followed the doctor's instructions exactly, instructing her each day to push the energy out of her liver, through her legs and paws, and put it down into the earth. I spoke to her directly and with great conviction. Everything I said, I fully believed was true. There was no doubt in me this healing would occur, because I never forgot something the author Wayne Dyer once said about our doubts being "our traitors."

In addition to the above daily routine, I made best efforts to ensure that Codi continued to eat nutritious food, including ample portions of the steamed vegetables she had grown to love over the years. Her nutritional program likewise included a double-dose each day of the Transfer Factor Canine Complete[4] supplement that Dr. Honey's friend, Tommy, had recommended. I decided to purchase it after doing some research on the Internet. Because it contained numerous vitamins, minerals, and other natural ingredients with healing properties, I felt it should be a part of her treatment program. Additionally, I continued to give Codi a daily dose of a supplement called Pet-Aloe® K-9 Crumbles[5] that we had been giving her for several years. Exercise, in the form of Frisbee sessions, also continued at least three times a day. The BC would have it no other way.

Everything seemed to be moving along splendidly, with one exception – she hadn't gained any of her weight back and the month of May was nearly over. In fact, she was thinner than ever and it surely wasn't from a lack of appetite or food. I couldn't understand it. I was *doing* all that I was supposed to do. I was focusing on what I wanted to manifest as opposed to concentrating on the original diagnosis (i.e., what I *didn't* want) and taking care of all the details of her treatment.

Being the analytical type, I carefully studied the situation and wondered what the problem was. The obvious answer was that I was expecting way too much too soon. Even so, were there any other critical actions that I needed to be taking? I remember thinking that if only Codi could talk, she could tell me if she needed something else. Wishful thinking, of course, but it was a thought that stuck with me for some reason.

With the arrival of June and the warmer weather, it soon became quite apparent that Codi didn't have the same stamina she'd had in the past. Even if the treatment effort was yielding positive results at some level, it was clear the illness was the primary culprit. The fact she had recently reached her 12th birthday could also have been a factor. Whatever the specific reason(s), it saddened me to see the look of frustration in her eyes when she wasn't able to work as much as she had in the past.

Witnessing her disappointment further strengthened my desire to reverse the course of her disease. There simply had to be something else I could do to help her! For some reason I was drawn to phone Lisa again, not to request healing assistance but just to share with her how I was feeling. As both a friend and a spiritual teacher, she had always been so very compassionate and kind to me. The truth was I needed Lisa's renowned big heart to lean on once again. When I finally got the opportunity to speak with her a few days later, as usual she listened attentively and with deep empathy to everything I said.

Throughout the course of our friendship, I learned again and again that Lisa could be counted on to serve as a reliable sounding board. This conversation was no exception. Of all that I shared with her, what she focused on was a phrase I apparently repeated a handful of times – "If only Codi could talk to me." Eventually, she said: "Did I tell you that earlier this year I paid for a session with a woman who specializes in animal communication?"

"No", I replied. "Do you mean like the pet psychic I've seen on Animal Planet?"

"Conceptually yes, she has the ability to communicate telepathically with animals, and also does healing work with them in the form of Reiki."

Lisa continued on to tell me she had hired this woman, whose name was Pam Sourelis, to work with her dog, Stas, regarding a behavioral issue he had developed. In particular, for no obvious reason he began hiding under the bed, and also became unresponsive to playtime. Lisa said she contacted Pam because nothing she did seemed to make any difference – not treats, new toys, or even more attention.

From just one session, Lisa learned that Stas' issues were the result of two house moves they had made in just six months. He didn't like the house where they were currently living, and, by no means wanted to stay there. With that insight in hand, Lisa was able to reassure him they wouldn't be there much longer. Thereafter, his behavior quickly returned to normal.

I know it's hard to believe what you just read, but try to keep an open mind. As I stated earlier, we know so little beyond the world of our five senses that we're simply not in a position to patently dismiss such claims. It seems unbelievable because *we* can't fathom having such a skill. Moreover, the idea of actually communicating with a dog in a conventional sense directly opposes what we have historically been taught about animal intelligence. Yet, what person who has a dog hasn't experienced occasions in which their pet has demonstrated some advanced intellect or awareness?

In these moments they appear to be truly sentient beings that demonstrate an identity or personality in a traditional way. Pam, it just so happens, apparently has the skill to somehow communicate with them; and, in the process, is able to assist them and their human caretakers. How she does it essentially doesn't matter *if*, in the end, the results are of benefit to them.

I really felt if Lisa and Stas were able to experience such success with her services, there was no reason we couldn't as well. Therefore, I was more than pleased to write down Pam's contact information and, in fact, I phoned her the very same day. We wound up having a great conversation, during which she highlighted her services, and also directed me to her website[6] to learn more about how she actually "does what she does."

Without hesitation, I chose to set up an appointment with her to meet with Codi one week later (July 9, 2004). I then spent the intervening week anxiously waiting to see what results that session would yield. Given Codi's consistent demonstrations of intelligence over the years, I honestly was expecting her to communicate very clearly with Pam.

13. *The First Conversation with Codi – July 9, 2004*

As the day finally arrived for Codi's session with Pam, I was filled with anticipation and a tiny bit of skepticism as well. Sure, Lisa had great success with her services, but the idea that a human being could literally *speak* to my dog was still somewhat of a stretch for me, even with my open-minded nature. I just hoped that something of value would result from the experience, perhaps some meaningful insight or at least some direction regarding the BC's condition.

What was most fascinating to me about the impending session was the fact it would take place remotely. Remarkably, Pam didn't need to spend time with Codi in person for, as referenced earlier, her type of communication was done telepathically. At the designated time, the only thing I needed to do was to ensure Codi wasn't eating or active in any way. Ideally, she was to be resting or, even better, sleeping. To ensure she was sufficiently mellow, just prior to the appointment I played with her for a few minutes inside the house.

Once she was a bit fatigued I put her toy away, she quickly went over to her water bowl for a drink, and then went into the living room to lie down and rest. At that point I took the opportunity to grab her gently by the snout, look straight into her eyes, and clearly explain to her what was going to happen that evening with Pam. I made it a point to ask her to please answer all of this woman's questions, and also to let Pam know anything else she felt was important for us to know.

The process was fairly straightforward – Pam was to call me at 7:00 p.m. and speak with me for a few minutes so as to fully understand the *purpose* of the session. Next, she would *meet* with Codi for 20–30 minutes and then call back to let me know what she had learned. When the phone rang at the agreed upon time, I was, of course, very eager to talk with her.

During our five minute chat I stated very clearly my objective for the session was to find out how Codi was feeling (i.e., was she in pain), and also to learn if there was anything else we could do to help her. I likewise reminded Pam about the original diagnosis, but provided no specific information regarding the treatment regimen I had been using for the past few weeks. Once that brief talk ended, I checked on Codi again and found her resting comfortably in the same place. For the next several minutes, I sat there quietly watching her and wondering what, if anything, she was communicating to Pam.

After what seemed like an hour, the phone finally rang. Picking it up nervously, I listened intently, feverishly scribbling down everything that Pam shared with me. The following *conversation* represents a simplified version[7] of the exchange of information that occurred between Pam and Codi that night:

Pam: Codi, I was asked by your human to communicate with you.

Codi: Yes, I knew you would be contacting me because he told me about you. What would you like to know?

Pam: Both of your humans are very concerned about you. Are you in any pain?

Codi: I am very aware of their concerns. Let them know that at this time I am feeling fine. I have no pain and feel completely at peace. I am aware of this disease in my body and I know it is going to progress.

Pam: Anything else that I should say to them?

Codi: Yes, tell him *he* is spending too much time and energy on his idea of *healing* me. These daily sessions are too much. I would rather that he just spends quiet time with me. He needs to lighten his own load and release his fears instead. The mass in my body is grief that I carry for others, and I am fine with this job. Tell him to stop asking me to put it down.

Pam: So you want him to focus on his life rather than yours?

Codi: Yes. He needs to put down the energies he himself carries that do not serve him. He must focus on his life lessons and leave mine to me.

Pam: But he loves you so much and doesn't want you to leave him.

Codi: I am well aware of this and naturally feel the same way. I am here to show him the connectedness of all beings. He still has much to learn in this area. The truth is I actually see him as a small child.

Pam: Is there anything else that he can do to help you at this time?

Codi: No. There is nothing more that can be done. He is caring for me perfectly. I am happy and quite serene. He needs to accept this is a path I have chosen and, once again, focus on his own lessons.

At this point Codi went silent, so Pam thanked her for the information and then ended the session.

14. July 9, 2004 – Meeting Aftermath

To say I was stunned by the contents of that first conversation would be an accurate statement. Whatever remaining skepticism I had about Pam's gift was removed when Codi requested that I, 'Stop asking her to put it down' (i.e., the cancer energy). While in our pre-session conversation I *did* mention Dr. Honey's suggestion about instructing Codi to push the energy out of her liver and put it down to the earth, I did *not* tell Pam I had been directing the BC to do that each morning for several weeks. Plus, Codi's statement about the mass in her body being grief she carries for others, closely matched how Dr. Honey had originally described it.

These facts made it obvious that somehow Codi did indeed communicate directly with Pam. At first I was so stunned by the experience that I didn't really focus much on what the BC specifically said about her condition. Instead, what grabbed my immediate attention were the paranormal aspects of the experience.

How could this have happened? It clearly defies logic. If I didn't already *know* it happened, I'd probably think it was a fictional story. But, I'm not making this stuff up! There is no explaining in common terms how an animal that chews on rawhide toys, and can't speak except in unintelligible barks, is able to communicate in such an in-depth and philosophical way with a human being.

Is it possible that dogs (and other animals) have a soul, a higher consciousness if you will? Do they take a so-called simpler life form for some specific reason? Are they perhaps like human beings, pieces of God consciousness in the process of evolving to higher levels of awareness? For domesticated dogs and cats as well, is part of their life plan to be in service in a deep way to their humans? Do we choose them or do they actually choose us? For several minutes that evening these questions and others like them raced through my mind. It took a bark by Heidi to snap me out of that reverie and back to reality.

From a pragmatic perspective, it really didn't matter how the information came to me. What was important was the information itself. Based on what Codi communicated, the news was very bad, indeed. For more than two months, I had been operating under the assumption that Codi shared my intense desire for her healing. Her conversation with Pam proved the fallacy of that notion. Now I was back to square one, my best friend had terminal cancer and there wasn't a damned thing I could do about it because, at some level, she, herself, had *chosen* it.

Along with this stark realization, a feeling of deep sorrow quickly resurfaced. It was as if a cloud of despair, coupled with a sense of powerlessness, had surrounded me. All my life I'd been a "make it happen" type person, but this time there was absolutely nothing I could do to *fix* this situation. The only option available to me was to continue to pour as much energy as possible into making her as comfortable as she could be under the circumstances.

As I filled Andrea in on all of this, we embraced, and then both of us began to cry. There was obviously no way of knowing how much longer Codi would be with us, nor did we have a clue as to precisely how the disease would run its course with respect to symptoms. We just had to make the best of a very bad situation. One thing was certain; I wouldn't hesitate to contact Pam again if we felt it was necessary to have additional insight from Codi about her condition.

15. July 10 – October 26, 2004

With full acceptance of Codi's terminal condition came an even more intense dedication to maximize her happiness and comfort during whatever time remained. The days of occasionally saying *no* to her requests to play were effectively over. And, when it came to food, we decided it was time to let her eat anything (within reason) that she was inspired to eat, providing it didn't serve to further aggravate her diseased liver.

One day early in this period, I remember commenting to a friend who worked for one of my clients that Codi was eating essentially whatever she wanted to and, "Last night it was Chunky Soup." Sadly, one of the other employees overhead my words and quipped with a chuckle, "Does she come right out and ask for it by brand name?" I was livid. The desire to get right up in his face about such insensitivity was overwhelming. Fortunately, in that moment my spiritual growth work apparently paid off. There would be no confrontation, because it would have served no purpose.

This individual, like many others, simply wasn't a dog person. While he was aware of Codi's illness, it never occurred to him that she was like a child to me, someone who meant every bit as much to me as his newest grandchild did to him. If you currently have (or have had) a close relationship with a dog, cat, or other type of companion animal, I'm certain you understand. Those who have never experienced the way animals can touch your heart are flat out unable to comprehend our feelings for them.

As the summer progressed it became increasingly apparent that Codi was slowly slipping away from us. Her spine was protruding even more and her ribs had begun to show clearly through her skin. In its march to its own demise, the cancer was consuming more and more of the nutrients in her body. It was also devouring the fat stored in her tissues, including the layer surrounding her eyes. This made her eye sockets fill with mucus and in the process, cloud her vision.

To overcome this, I sterilized an old eyedropper and used it to suction the mucus from the corners of both eyes. Codi's initial response to this wasn't very positive but, once she realized it helped to improve her vision, she was fine with it. Some days it was necessary for me to do it perhaps three to four times and, as the illness worsened, this number grew as well.

The BC's appetite likewise continued a slow descent that required us to be increasingly creative in order to inspire her to eat. The fragile condition of her liver, however, meant for certain we could not feed her excessively fatty foods. Moreover, the days of her being able to eat just about anything at all were undoubtedly over. For example, no longer could she handle an occasional bite or two of cantaloupe and several other foods she loved, as eating them would result in intestinal problems. And, since this condition would sometimes affect her quite unexpectedly and rapidly, no matter what she ate, accidents inside the house occasionally occurred as the summer wore on. While such events were an inconvenience for us, they were just devastating to Codi. The way her ears turned back and her head slumped it was obvious she was truly embarrassed by what she had done. I can imagine how horribly she felt because it wasn't something she would *ever* have done in the past.

By the time the fall arrived, Codi's weight had fallen to 30 pounds from roughly 40 back in February. The primary effect of this was the loss of muscle mass in her legs, and in turn reduced stability and agility. This led to a key turning point in her life as it became necessary for us to bring an end her outdoor Frisbee sessions. Though this deeply saddened me and clearly frustrated her, there really was no other choice following an event that occurred in late September. One day she tried to complete a quick pivot to chase the disk and then instantly crumpled down in a heap. Clearly startled, she slowly rose to her feet indicating that she was OK, but the look in her eyes seemed to say, "Dad, why can't I do what I used to do anymore?" That incident, however, combined with another in which she was accidentally bumped into by Heidi and easily knocked to the ground, convinced me it just wasn't safe for her to play in the open spaces anymore.

While I really missed playing Frisbee with her, the progression of the disease made this the only sensible option. This didn't mean no more play time whatsoever, for Codi would *never* stand for that. From her perspective, I'm certain she'd have rather been dead than not be able to play at all. So, we just switched gears a bit and focused on indoor play sessions instead. To ensure she wasn't tempted to be a "hot dog," her beloved Frisbee was replaced by a squeaky toy made of soft rubber. Unlike the disk, it didn't float in unpredictable ways that would require her to make any sudden moves and risk falling down.

In spite of her declining health, Codi continued to demand to play several times a day. The ritual was always the same, I'd sit in my office and toss the toy into our bedroom and she'd gingerly trot after it. Then she would return it, squeaking it the entire time. After a few tosses, I'd take it away and she'd protest a tad before settling down to sleep. When I had to work away from my home office, Andrea would take over my role.

One of our key objectives was to keep her daily life routine as close as possible to what it had always been. For the most part we achieved this goal, and each day did our best not to look beyond the present. This was perhaps one of the most profound lessons we learned from her during this entire process – how to stay focused in the "now." While even today I continue to struggle in applying it, thanks primarily to this experience with Codi, I've at least learned to be more aware of when I'm "time traveling."

As the month of October waned we were very pleased the BC had lived over six full months since the original diagnosis. Based on both the apparent stability of her condition, and her powerful will to keep living, in some sense we actually felt optimistic about her longevity. We had, unfortunately, lost track of the old admonition that in a New York minute, anything can change.

16. October 27, 2004

This day started like any other as we went about our usual morning rituals. I was slated to work outside the home office so Andrea was totally responsible for Codi's care. I left about 9:00 a.m. and expected to return after six in the evening. I knew the BC was in excellent hands but, at that stage in her life, the grim reality was that her days were numbered. So being away from her at all was something I really hated to do.

Work was intense, as usual, and the hours passed quickly. Around 4:00 p.m., I was told Andrea was on the phone. As soon as I heard that, I jumped up to grab the call outside the conference room a group of us were using. While it was common for her to phone me at the office, I recall my first words to her were, "What's wrong?"

With a quivering voice, she said "It's Codi. She's lying on the living floor and won't get up to go outside. Right after lunch she started acting strange and then had a couple of accidents. It all happened so fast, Jeff, but I finally got her outside about 2:00 and she started squatting, and then did it again and again for several minutes."

"Then what happened?"

"When she came in, I cleaned her up and scrubbed the carpet as well. I also tried to get her to take some water. She refused, then stretched out on the floor and went to sleep."

"Is she conscious?"

"Yes, she just won't move. *Please* come home as soon as you can."

I told her I'd do my best, and hung up the phone. As I returned to the meeting I was visibly quite upset. As people had come from all over the country to attend this session, I really didn't have the option to simply get up and leave. Nonetheless, my thoughts kept shifting back to Codi during the rest of the afternoon, and time moved very slowly as a result. The meeting finally broke up at about 5:30, which allowed me to return home a bit after six to find Codi lying in the same spot Andrea mentioned. As I approached her tail began a slow, steady thump against the floor. 'A good sign,' I thought, so I bent down for a closer look. My sense was she had exhausted herself in the process of dealing with her intestinal difficulties.

Out of habit I asked her if she was okay and told her it would be best for her to get up and get moving. I also let her know I was going to pick her up to go outside. I did so and she didn't struggle at all. After placing her down in the front yard I supported her weight to make sure she didn't fall down. She was able to take a few staggering steps before squatting to do her business. This also was a good sign but it didn't address the problem of her exhaustion. We decided at once to make a phone call to our veterinarian, Dr. Laura Clarke.

Since it was well after office hours, we had no choice but to try and reach Laura at home. Months earlier, she had kindly volunteered her personal number, indicating that we should feel free to phone her at any time. This sincere interest in her patients is a trademark of Laura's treatment approach. The deep compassion she had whenever she interacted with Codi (or Heidi) was patently obvious to anyone in the room at the time. Although she wasn't home when I phoned, she promptly returned my call. After thanking her profusely, I explained what had occurred that day. Laura's immediate diagnosis confirmed my initial instincts – *dehydration.*

"You simply must get her to drink a large quantity of water, Jeff," she said.

"I tried to force her to do so but she's not going for it."

"You have to keep the pressure on her because the fluids are a critical part of detoxification, particularly so in her case, given the diseased nature of her liver."

"Okay I'll make another attempt to persuade her after we hang up. Before I forget, do you have any time in your schedule tomorrow?"

"Just bring her in about 10:00 a.m. and we'll squeeze her in."

I thanked her again and ended the call.

Turning to Codi once more, it was obviously time for another "father-daughter" chat. I moved in close to her and slowly explained why she needed to drink some water. After her first session with Pam, I was now more certain than ever that she understood exactly what I said, and hoped she would honor my request. I lifted her up from the bedroom floor, carried her to the kitchen, and placed her down near her water bowl, making sure to steady her as she stood. Her initial response was to ignore the water, but with a bit more encouragement she finally lapped up a small amount. After some additional prompting, she took a smidge more before turning away. 'That was a start at least,' I thought. She would have a small amount more at bedtime but not nearly enough to offset all the fluids she lost earlier in the day. The truth was she probably was just too tired to go through the act of drinking.

The good news was that we were going to see Dr. Clarke the next day. I was confident Laura could do *something* to help her. As I lay in bed that night, my mind was focused on one thought – How could I get her to drink more water?

17. October 28, 2004

We left about 9:00 a.m. for the vet's office, leaving Heidi
at home so as not to complicate the situation. Thankfully,
Codi made it through the night without any recurrence
of the previous day's symptoms. Nevertheless, she was still
very tired and quite sluggish as well. While she had a small
amount of water prior to our departure, it still was not
nearly enough to get her adequately hydrated. As we drove
the 35 miles she slept peacefully on a blanket in the back
seat. This was just the second time in her entire life she
didn't stand up to check out the scenery.

Once we arrived, it wasn't long before we were led to
the examining room where Dr. Clarke was to meet with
us. Codi promptly stretched out on the floor, panting
slowly and looking somewhat disoriented. As soon as Laura
saw the BC her facial expression changed dramatically. The
last time she had set eyes on her was eight months earlier,
which was two months prior to the cancer diagnosis being
made at a different animal hospital. While we had spoken
about her condition over the phone, it was, quite obviously, a shock for Laura to see just how much her physical
stature had changed in such a short time. As Laura knelt
down on the floor to greet her, Codi's tail thumped a few
times and she licked her hand a bit. Laura then completed
a basic exam, including checking her weight, which was 30
percent less than it was at the time of her last visit.

The exam confirmed her initial suspicion that Codi
had a case of severe dehydration resulting from the intestinal issues she experienced the previous day. She explained

that giving fluids intravenously would require hospitalization to ensure safe and proper delivery. Since this was something we really didn't want Codi to experience at this stage in her life, we asked if there was another alternative. Laura then recommended giving her a bag of fluids by inserting a needle in a general area of tissue. This approach would allow for faster absorption of the fluids and, hopefully, would enable her to bounce back somewhat. Because of our faith in Laura's judgment, we naturally agreed to go forward with that treatment option. A vet technician was promptly summoned to assist with the process, which would take perhaps 20–30 minutes.

After the therapy began, Laura sat down and said, "I want you to understand there is no guarantee this will provide any long term benefits. She *may* get a nice bounce from this, but the next 36 hours or so will tell the tale. Because I hadn't seen her since she was diagnosed I must admit I was somewhat taken aback by my first glimpse of her. Based on the weight loss alone, the cancer has progressed substantially."

"Yes," I replied, "I could tell by the look on your face that you were a bit stunned by the change in her appearance."

"I see this in my work all too often and it never gets any easier. I know how much she means to you two so I can imagine how difficult this must be for you. I'm so very sorry."

We thanked her for her kindness and, after dabbing away a few tears, I asked, "What do you think about her prospects for overcoming this current setback?"

"There's no way to know for certain, of course," she replied, "but I really feel if she doesn't show signs of increased energy and appetite by Saturday, you might have to make a very difficult decision to let her go."

Hearing those words, I was both shocked and scared. 'Surely,' I thought, 'this could not be the end for her.' I simply wouldn't accept this – not yet anyway. I *knew* she could overcome this obstacle. "Laura, I have every confidence this treatment can turn her around, but what else can we do over the next few days to increase the chances that it will?"

She replied, "You must do your best to hydrate her even more. Find some way to motivate her to drink more water. You might also try to give her some Pedialyte. You can find it at any drugstore or pharmacy."

"Thanks for the advice. We'll definitely purchase some. The problem is how do we get her to drink something when she doesn't want to? She's pretty strong-willed you know."

"Knowing you, I'm certain you'll figure something out."

Before we knew it, 25 minutes had passed and the treatment was finished. Thankfully, Codi perked up nicely and had a much healthier look to her as well. We thanked Laura for all the time she spent with us then hugged her goodbye. As I was paying the bill at the reception desk, she came out once more to remind me we should continue to feel free to phone her at home again if need be. I expressed my gratitude again, said goodbye, and headed out to the car where Andrea and Codi were waiting. On the way home we both remarked how very blessed we felt to have a vet like Laura.

When we were about halfway home the BC resumed

her normal behavior of standing up in the back seat, which was, indeed, a very encouraging sign. While driving I continued to grapple with the challenge of getting her to drink more, including the Pedialyte Laura had recommended. Then, seemingly out of nowhere the idea to use a turkey baster suddenly dawned on me. When I mentioned this idea to Andrea, she smiled at the novelty of it and agreed with me that we should at least give it a try once we got her home and settled in.

Pulling into the driveway, it took just a split second for Heidi to start barking in her usual frenzied manner. As soon as I lifted Codi out of the car, she walked slowly and deliberately to the back door of the garage, indicating she was ready to play. 'Amazing,' I thought. 'Old habits sure do die hard.' Once Andrea let Heidi out and both dogs did their usual sniff-sniff, the pups and I went inside for lunch while Andrea headed to the local pharmacy to buy some Pedialyte. After eating, Codi promptly laid down to take a nap, which wasn't a surprise given the stress she dealt with during the previous 24 hours.

When she awoke later that afternoon, I decided to experiment with using the turkey baster for giving her the Pedialyte. Prior to doing so, I explained to her precisely what I was going to do and why. I also asked her to *please* swallow as much as she could handle. Codi looked at me very intensely in her customary manner, giving the usual impression that she was paying full attention to every word. Standing above her with my legs on either side to steady her, I carefully inserted the baster inside her lower lip area near the back of her mouth, lightly squirted a small amount of the liquid into her mouth and gently said, "swallow." Although she certainly had the option to spit it out, she instead chose to obey the command. Within a few minutes she had finished a 12-ounce serving, visibly demonstrating she was by no means ready to give up on life.

Thanks to Codi's determination there would be no need after all for a return trip to see Dr. Clarke the following Saturday. It took just a handful of hours (not 36) for us to reach that conclusion. She had survived her first serious health challenge since being diagnosed with liver cancer and, based upon her turnaround this time, we soon felt optimistic again regarding her ability to handle others as the disease progressed. Her willingness to comply with my command to drink from the turkey baster didn't surprise me though. In general, being obedient was another one of her trademarks.

18. Codi's Obedience – January 1996

Border Collies are always very competitive when it comes to participating in obedience trials, because their natural intelligence and intensity make them very trainable. Other than the rare times when they are purposely being impudent (see Chapter 19), you can easily tell they really do want to please in every way possible. While animal intelligence experts say that no dog actually "thinks" in the manner of a sentient being, I'm not so sure. There were many times in Codi's life when her obedience exceeded even the loftiest of my expectations.

One incident I will always remember occurred during January of 1996, about a week after our second dog, Heidi, joined the family. A rescue dog from a local shelter, Heidi was a six month old Border Collie mix who needed training in all respects. Codi, at nearly four years old, already had mastered all of her lessons. By that time, we had become quite accustomed to the ease of dealing with a fully-trained Border Collie who could be trusted on her own out in the yard.

It was my fervent hope that Codi would assist in the training process by setting an example, showing Heidi *how* to behave. What I didn't know was that Heidi wouldn't follow the new behavioral pattern of a fellow pack member until she had accepted Codi as the alpha dog. Naively, I assumed the younger dog would simply fall into line behind the older one. So, for roughly the first couple of weeks there was constant (though not intense) conflict between these two females jockeying for position.

About ten days into the new "pack" dynamics, I made a critical error in judgment. One evening I assumed Heidi could be trusted off-lead in the front yard. For whatever reason, I felt she had seen enough of Codi's outdoor behavior for it to be imprinted into her consciousness. Suffice it to say, the assumption was wrong, completely wrong. The moment I unclipped her from the lead she took off like a jackrabbit heading east up the street. Compounding the problem of it being dark and very cold outside (20 degrees Fahrenheit), the identification tag we had ordered for Heidi a week earlier still hadn't arrived. If someone other than I were to find her, there obviously would be no way to know to whom she belonged.

Seeing her gallop away, there was no other choice but to take off after her as quickly as possible. In the bat of an eye I turned to look at Codi, stared directly into her eyes and said in a firm voice, "Sit and stay right here, and don't you move until I come back." She immediately sat, as commanded, and I wheeled around and started running up the street to search for Heidi.

Filled with adrenaline, I ran flat out for perhaps a half-minute until an outline of what appeared to be Heidi appeared in the distance. Sure enough, she was standing in the front yard of a house perhaps a block away. Getting closer to her, I called her name but instead of coming to see me she took off running again. This time she turned south, with me following as quickly as possible in pursuit. Finally, after about two blocks, she paused to sniff a bit in some backyard. Whatever got her attention held it long enough for me to sneak up within about ten feet of her. Getting down on my hands and knees, I slowly crawled toward her while continually calling her name in a very soft tone. After a minute or so had passed I got close enough to grab her by the collar and attach the lead. Mission accomplished and lesson learned.

Looking at my watch, I noted it had been more than ten minutes since I left Codi alone at home in the front yard. While I wasn't concerned about her running away, I did want to get home ASAP since, at a minimum, she might be getting a bit cold as well as impatient with the situation. As Heidi and I approached the house, I looked closely to see if Codi was anywhere near where she was earlier. Much to my amazement, she was sitting in the *exact same spot* as when the sit-stay command was given. She literally hadn't moved an inch in more than ten minutes. That, my dear Reader, was an extreme example of her obedience.

To this day, I remain astounded that she adhered to that command so literally. Codi, however, took it all in stride, to the point of virtually ignoring all of the praise we heaped upon her that night.

19. Codi's Impudence

So far in what I've shared with you, Codi obviously comes across in a very positive way. After all, why would anyone take the time to write a book about their dog primarily to point out its negative characteristics? The reality is, however, just like every human being, each dog has its imperfections. And, of course, each behaves poorly at times. Codi certainly was no exception. In her case, though, I eventually came to believe the slips in her behavior weren't the least bit accidental. When she misbehaved, it was in a very deliberate way.

An excellent example of this occurred during *November 1992*. Andrea and I had decided to attend her 10-year high school reunion and this required that we leave Codi in someone else's care, since the event was to take place 150 miles away in Champaign, Illinois. This would be the first time she would be apart from us for an entire night. To ensure she had proper care, I made arrangements with a neighbor to feed her and let her out around 6:00 p.m. Later that night, a friend agreed to stay the night at our house, with the plan being for him to arrive about 9:00 p.m. and leave early the next morning. Our intention was to return home by noon that day to make sure she had her mid-day meal on time.

As we said our goodbyes that day, both of us felt sad about leaving and perhaps a little guilty as well. As she stared out at us in the car from her perch in the living room window, the look in Codi's eyes mirrored that sadness. Driving away, I felt a twinge of worry about the arrangements I made for her care. What if something happened to the neighbor or the overnight dogsitter? How would she feel with us not there for her an entire night? Would she be afraid? Would she feel abandoned if the other two members of her "pack" disappeared so suddenly? It would certainly be understandable, given we had been with her every single day and night for nearly five months. I could only hope she'd adjust, for there was no going back.

At the reunion I did my best to remain confident that all was going well back home. The folks I asked to help us were reliable and responsible individuals and I also had left a number where we could be reached, just in case something went awry. 'What could possibly go wrong,' I thought. While I don't give much credence to Murphy's Law, we've all experienced times when things don't work out despite our best efforts to ensure otherwise.

In this particular instance, unfortunately the person who had agreed to spend the night with Codi flat out forgot to show up! If it wasn't for the fact that both of her water bowls were empty, we wouldn't have known this the following day when we arrived home. If he had actually stayed overnight, it's unlikely he would have left in the morning without filling them. One thing was certain, there was no way Codi would have emptied them both between nine in the morning and noon when we made it home.

Interestingly, everything else in the house appeared to be in fine order. There were no messes and nothing was damaged. It was as if we hadn't left for more than a few minutes. Nonetheless, another clue we had indicating she had been left alone was the way she totally ignored us when we entered the house. She essentially gave us no greeting at all, but instead ran to the front door barking aggressively to be let outside. Once there, she went immediately to do her business which, for obvious reasons, took a lot longer than usual. When she came back inside she went tearing into our bedroom where Andrea was unpacking. I followed her there, and it was at that moment Codi let us know *exactly* how she felt about our absence the previous evening.

Despite having emptied her bladder just minutes before, she stood directly in front of us, squatted down and urinated again! Both of us were totally stunned by this act. After all, this was a dog who had originally mastered house-training in less than two weeks. My immediate response was to scold her for such out-of-character behavior. It was only after things calmed down again that I came to the conclusion the act was deliberate. It was her way of showing her disappointment with us in a very dramatic manner.

Over the course of her time with us, Codi actually demonstrated an impudent nature on a fairly regular basis. Another telling example was her insistence on getting play-time even after having been told "no" very sternly. As I've indicated in earlier chapters, Codi was totally obsessed with play (or to her, *work*), so much so there eventually came a point where we had to remove her toys from the floor and hide them inside one of our closets. Leaving a toy or ball in plain sight meant we would constantly have to reach down and toss it or she'd do something annoying (e.g., see fake bark earlier in Chapter 6) to remind us to do so.

Initially, the closet became an ideal solution. Once the door was closed, she'd quickly get the picture and back off her demands. It didn't take long, however, for this solution to lose its effectiveness. Codi soon learned how to get past this particular bi-fold door by punching it firmly with one of her front paws in precisely the right place to cause it to open ever so slightly. Then, she used her snout to slide the door fully open, after which she easily could enter and grab her toy of choice. Once again, she knew *exactly* what she was doing and did it in spite of repeatedly being told "No, bad girl!"

Although some dog training expert, like Cesar on the National Geographic cable TV channel, could likely have stopped this behavior and left the toys in the closet, we chose another approach – we just moved them to the top of the refrigerator! This was a far simpler approach than getting into a battle of wills with a very headstrong and intelligent Border Collie. Of course, even that approach needed to be refined a bit, because she soon learned to sit in the kitchen, stare at the toys on the fridge and bark until we gave in again and allowed her to do what *she* wanted. The only way we ever got past this was first to distract her attention and then hide the toys in yet another location.

Looking back, to think that a 40-pound dog could so control two adult humans is actually quite comical. She truly did have a mind of her own and wasn't the least bit shy about taking control of situations. In her case, there was a thin line between intelligence and impudence and she tiptoed along it her entire life. One day she could dazzle you with her ability to learn a new, complicated skill within just a few repetitions. The next day she could aggravate you by stealing food off your plate!

In this regard, I'll never forget the time Andrea had an almost eaten blueberry muffin next to her on the couch while she was sipping coffee and watching TV. In the blink of an eye, not a single crumb was left and the wrapper had disappeared as well. This occurred despite the fact we trained her as a puppy not to behave in such a manner. While she never had done this before and never did it again, this was, evidently, just a time when she saw a golden opportunity and simply *had* to take advantage of it!

After hearing this type of story, some might say we did a lousy job of training her. But, the truth was she didn't *always* misbehave. She only did so when she felt like pushing the envelope a bit. Over time, I actually came to enjoy her impudence because, despite the momentary annoyance the behavior caused, in the end it usually brought a smile to my face. Moreover, I came to appreciate the challenges associated with having such an intelligent, yet obstinate dog. She made things interesting each day and that made for a more stimulating life around our home. Codi may not have been an impeccably trained dog but she certainly was a perfect dog for us.

20. December 2004 – January 22, 2005

As December began Codi's weight had dropped to only 25 pounds, causing even more deterioration of the muscle mass in her legs. Walking, therefore, became much more challenging and ascending the front steps intimidated her. With about two weeks left before Christmas, she finally reached the point where she refused even to attempt it. This left us with no other choice but to carry her back in each time she needed to go outside. We also had to continue to ensure Heidi didn't accidentally bang into her since, in her weakened state, any fall could result in a serious injury.

When Codi walked on carpeting she was relatively stable and safe. The same could not be said for the hardwood floor in my office and the tile floor in the kitchen. After a couple of incidents in which she slipped and fell while returning her toy to me in the office, I decided to place a carpet runner diagonally across the hardwood floor. This enabled her to safely deliver the toy to me for another toss into the bedroom. As frail as she had become, I continued to be amazed at her determination to keep working in some manner. Providing she maintained such a strong will to live, we would go on supporting her in any way we could.

A week before Christmas, we decided to purchase a tree and decorate it in our usual fashion. While I was stringing the lights, I couldn't help but trend into thoughts about this being the last holiday season she would spend with us. Though I tried my best not to give much energy to such thoughts, the progression of the illness since October could not be denied. Living one day at a time had been our focus for several months. Even though we had done a respectable job in maintaining this posture, occasionally we found ourselves wondering when the proverbial "other shoe" would drop. Sadly, one morning a couple of weeks after Christmas, it did.

We awoke this particular day to find Codi unable to walk at all on her right front leg. Upon closer examination, there didn't *appear* to be anything obviously wrong with her paw. So, I tried vigorously rubbing that leg as a means of getting the blood moving a bit more. Regrettably, this did nothing to solve the problem. If she was at full strength, she could potentially adapt by hopping around. However, the cancer and the weight loss had sapped her strength far too much. This was, therefore, a life-threatening situation for her. If she couldn't move, she'd have no ability to play, and accordingly, no quality of life on her terms.

In that moment, the most pressing concern was to get her outside to take care of her business. Andrea suggested using a bath towel to support her weight and move her around the yard. I did precisely that, and Codi promptly got the picture by quickly doing what she needed to do. After carrying her inside and settling her in again, I knew it was time to phone Dr. Clarke again at the animal hospital. Luckily, she was between patients and took the call immediately.

Once aware of the symptoms, she advised me to closely examine every square inch of the leg in question to try and identify *anything* that might appear abnormal. I put her on hold a minute in order to do exactly as she said. It wasn't long before I identified a small growth near the first metacarpal joint, just above the paw. Touching this growth with any firmness caused her to pull the leg out of my grasp with some force.

After reporting this to Laura, her first impression was that an infection of some type had developed. To avoid putting Codi through the stress of a long ride to the animal hospital, she offered instead to prescribe an antibiotic. I thanked her and then provided the necessary contact information for her to phone in the prescription. Before hanging up, Laura also recommended I make an attempt to put some pressure on the growth, as it might just be a sebaceous cyst that would drain on its own. I told her I'd give it a try, and we said our goodbyes.

While Andrea went to the drug store to pick up the prescription, I sat down on the floor with the BC and again looked closely at her leg. Isolating the growth, I began to lightly squeeze it. She stirred a bit at first, but after a few words from me she calmed down. I then applied even more intense pressure and, suddenly, a rush of yellowish liquid squirted from the growth. Putting more force on it caused even more fluid to be released, along with a fair amount of blood. With that complete, I cleaned the leg with soap and water and, then applied an ice pack to help reduce the swelling. As soon as Andrea returned, I filled her in on our progress and gave Codi her first dose of the antibiotic.

By later that evening she was walking on that leg again and, though I had to drain the growth several more times over the next few days, the fact remained she had dodged another bullet. Her cooperation throughout this episode demonstrated yet another time just how determined she was to cling to life. It truly was a powerfully inspirational event to witness. Compare this approach to our own human tendency to take life for granted and it makes one wonder which species has the more satisfying life.

In my experience, dogs and other animals appear more capable of innately appreciating life itself. Therefore, perhaps their outward appearance of being unable to think and reason like us isn't such a disadvantage after all. When not feeling well, they aren't burdened with thoughts like, "this isn't fair," or "why is this happening to me?" Instead, they just instinctively trust in the life force that created them and flow with whatever they are experiencing. There are times I really envy them for that ability to just "be" without analyzing and evaluating everything. Try as I may, it's very rare that I can actually even come close to being that focused in the "now."

By the third week of January, Codi was walking again without any problems. The cyst had completely healed to the point where she could get back to playing gingerly with her toy. Naturally, we were very grateful for her recovery and hoped her condition would remain stable for a while at least. Fortunately this turned out to be the case but, a few days later, a new, annoying behavior on her part suddenly appeared, presenting us with yet another obstacle to overcome.

Literally out of the blue one night, just after we turned out the lights to go to sleep, Codi began barking for no apparent reason. There was no potential threat for, if there was, Heidi surely would have been yapping like crazy.

No, this was just a slow, monotonous sound that continued despite repeated commands for her to stop. As I mentioned earlier, Codi wasn't typically a very vocal dog, so this behavior was really unusual.

Andrea and I were both very tired and, as such, quite frustrated with the situation. After about an hour of her chirping away, the point was finally reached where I simply couldn't stand it anymore. Frustration boiled over to anger and I decided to pick both Codi and her dog bed up and place them in the bathroom on the other side of the house. Plugging a nightlight in, I told her she had to stay in there because her barking was driving us nuts. Afterwards I bent down and kissed her on her forehead, said "I'm sorry," then closed the bathroom door along with the door to our bedroom.

As the old saying goes, we were fit to be tied with this new and very infuriating behavior. We knew there had to be a reason for it and, after several days of wondering about its origin, we finally came to the conclusion that another session with Pam (the animal communicator) definitely was necessary.

21. *Codi Speaks Again –*
January 23, 2005

To get to the bottom of Codi's annoying new bedtime barking habit, I arranged for Pam to meet with her again. The process was the same as the earlier session in that the communication took place on a remote basis, with Pam phoning me once it was completed. As I noted earlier in Chapter 13, the following *conversation* represents a simplified version of the exchange of information that occurred between Pam and Codi on this particular night:

Pam: Codi, your humans are again very concerned about how you are feeling.

Codi: Yes, I know this. I am not going to be here much longer but I have things to *tell* them!

Pam: Is it about pain? Are you in pain right now?

Codi: No, I am not experiencing any currently. I just feel that I'm slowly slipping away. This saddens me deeply because I love life and don't want to leave.

Pam: I understand. Is this why you've started barking late at night?

Codi: Yes. I'm trying to tell them that I want them to live every moment! To suck every morsel out of life before it's gone. I want him to know my barking is about his unrealized dreams. He needs to know there is no tomorrow, only *now*. He needs to stop being so impatient about these unrealized dreams and instead focus on becoming fully present in his life!

Pam: I will be certain to emphasize this to him. Is there anything they can do to make *you* more comfortable?

Codi: No! I am fine. I have no complaints.

Pam: You said earlier you had little time left. Would you like them to assist you in leaving your physical body?

Codi: No. I prefer to leave on my own. Just tell them to be patient with me.

As with their first visit, at this point Codi went silent, so Pam thanked her for the information and then ended the session.

22. *January 23, 2005 – Meeting 11 Aftermath*

In our follow-up conversation, Pam pointed out that Codi was *different* during this meeting. She was less vocal but very determined in her tone. It was critical to her that Pam emphasize the importance of her message regarding the need for me to be more "present" in my life. Just like the previous session, Codi shared information that was highly relevant to both my personal and spiritual growth. The first time I was somewhat stunned by the experience itself. On this occasion, I immediately focused on the information she shared.

The fact that she wasn't experiencing any pain was particularly comforting. We also were relieved to learn she didn't want us to help her leave, as the thought of making the decision to put her to sleep terrified us. The mere idea of standing there and watching her die was simply too disturbing to even consider. Like anyone else with a beloved animal companion, as the illness progressed, we hoped against hope that when the time came for her to go, it would happen peacefully in her sleep.

As I reflected more deeply on this latest conversation with her, the admonition about living life to the fullest really slapped me upside the head. Throughout my adult life, I have had an inclination for worrying about the future and, during the preceding 18 months or so, I had taken this proclivity to an even greater extreme. This anxiety was related to the release of my first book, *Spirituality Simplified*[8], because ever since the decision was made to self-publish the initial print run, I was pretty much obsessed with the book's sales progress.

At the time, the truth was my dream of quick market acceptance for the book had not been realized. As such, my thoughts were highly focused on this unrealized dream and others related to it. Amazingly, *my dog* was keenly aware of this and very concerned about how it was distracting me from fully enjoying my life in the present moment. Without a doubt, Codi's terminal condition put her in a position where she was particularly sensitive to the importance of living in the "now."

Once again, the session with Pam was worthwhile in many respects. We were very grateful for the information she relayed to us and quite certain we would be calling on her again before too long.

23. January 24, 2005 – March 31, 2005

Although Codi told Pam she still wasn't in any pain, the fact was her condition was noticeably deteriorating. One of the obvious indications was that it had become increasingly difficult to motivate her to eat each day. With her liver functioning at such a reduced level, the viable food options available were indeed very limited. As such, she continued to lose weight, further reducing both her energy level and mobility.

This stage of the illness likewise was marked by a tendency for more accidents in the house, as she had less and less control of her bowels. This was by no means a daily occurrence for, if it were, we would have had little choice but to assist her in leaving. Nevertheless, the times such mishaps did happen had a devastating effect on the carpeting installed in most of the house. But, given all the joy she brought to us during the course of our years together, cleaning up after her and providing her with hospice type care at the close of her life was the very least I could do.

As bad as I felt about the clean-up episodes, however, they disturbed Codi far more. In those instances when they happened right in front of me, the look in her eyes clearly reflected the shame and embarrassment she felt. Since I knew the behavior wasn't in any way intentional, I did my best to comfort her first before moving on to dealing with the problem.

By this point in the BC's life, it also became necessary for me to carry her *down* the front stairs whenever she needed to go out. I likewise needed to remain right next to her to provide physical support while she completed her business, as her legs had weakened to the point where it was quite difficult for her to assume a squat position. When she'd finish, I'd carry her back up the steps and into the house. Occasionally, a neighbor would see us out in the front yard and stop to stare for a moment or two. A part of me felt awkward about that because by no means did I want to leave the impression we were trying to extend her life on our behalf.

One particular day when I placed her down in the front yard, I let go a bit too soon and she fell. A couple of folks who live across the street saw what happened and they looked very sad as they watched her struggling to get up by herself. I couldn't help but believe Codi caught a glimpse of them pitying her, so from that point forward, each time we went outside I walked further into the yard and put her down behind a hedge where she couldn't be easily seen.

Another time, a different neighbor who had crossed the street to check her mailbox approached me after she saw Codi staggering a bit while walking toward the front steps. Once we exchanged pleasantries, she felt compelled to advise me it was perhaps time for us to put her down because, in her current condition, she couldn't be having any quality of life. Moreover, she commented something to the effect that we shouldn't be selfish enough to keep her alive for ourselves when she was obviously suffering.

Internally, my first reaction was to lash out and tell her to mind her own business. Instead, I opted to take a deep breath before replying that I appreciated her input.

I then added that things weren't as dire as they appeared. In that moment, I could have chosen to provide her with examples of Codi's continuing strong will to live, but honestly felt no need to explain myself further. And, since there was no practical sense in telling a casual acquaintance about the BC's statement to Pam that she wasn't yet experiencing any pain, I merely assured her there was no way I would keep Codi alive if I *knew*, for a fact, she was suffering. The simple truth is, the decision to put a pet down is a difficult one. Unless a person is witness to all aspects of the situation, there's no way they can possibly know the proper course of action to take at any point in the process.

While not knowing *exactly* how Codi was feeling at this stage was very frustrating, the only sensible option was to trust the information Pam had relayed from her last session with the BC. Nonetheless, I carefully monitored her condition each day in an effort to discern whether she actually was experiencing any discomfort. Something that caught my attention during the middle part of February was a fairly loud gurgling sound emanating from her abdomen each time she finished eating. This was not your typical grumbling tummy noise but actually sounded quite sinister in nature. I could only assume this was the cancer growing and impinging upon her digestive organs. A call to our vet, Dr. Clarke, confirmed this was likely the case, with worst news being that the processes underlying the sound ultimately would lead to some very significant pain.

One thing remaining essentially status quo during this time period was Codi's desire for play. Although her physical abilities were severely diminished, she maintained a strong interest in chasing and retrieving her favorite squeaky toy. To ensure she didn't slip and fall while playing on the hardwood floor in my office, I kept the previously mentioned carpet runner in place between my office and the doorway to our bedroom. What was particularly interesting to me was how aware she was of her limitations. She no longer moved quickly after the toy, instead she chose to walk slowly back and forth.

These play sessions occurred several times a day for fairly short periods. As long as she maintained her dedication to working, I could see no reason why I shouldn't continue to indulge her. Looking back, it's obvious these times served to demonstrate that Codi was doing exactly what she had told Pam to admonish *us* to do – sucking every morsel out of life before it was gone. Seeing this frail little dog so committed to living life to the fullest, in spite of her significant physical shortcomings, was incredibly inspirational to both of us. We literally were awed by her courage. The lessons learned by witnessing how tenaciously she clung to life and how committed she was to living life on her terms, certainly will remain with us forever.

As I stated earlier, unlike human beings who *evaluate* the conditions affecting them, then make corresponding judgments about these conditions (e.g., this is unfair, why me?), dogs just go with the flow, making the best of their circumstances at every moment. Since, for centuries, spiritual teachers have emphasized the importance of staying in the "now" as a means of fostering happiness, it is not unreasonable to assert that the dog is actually the spiritually superior species.

Strongly religious people might take serious issue with this contention, though it is, in my view, a position that has merit. Why? Because dogs' ability to stay firmly focused in the present moment enables them to maintain a much stronger connection to the energy of the God-force itself, an energy that is *always* focused in the "now."

Although I greatly admired Codi for her spiritual superiority, for her will to live and her bravery in dealing with such a horrible illness, I must admit that one particular behavior during this period consistently tested my ability to remain patient and loving with her. Namely, she continued her recently-acquired habit of barking each night soon after the lights went out for bed. I had hoped she would stop doing this after Pam delivered her message to me about my dropping my tendency to focus on "unrealized dreams." Such was not the case.

Despite doing everything I could to comfort her, including blowing up an air mattress one night so I could sleep next to her on the floor, the annoying behavior re-emerged each night. At first, I refused to just lock her in the bathroom on the other side of the house when bedtime arrived. I hoped that, given the chance to stay with us or get locked up again, she eventually would decide to stop. While some nights she actually did remain quiet for a spell, this was merely a brief respite before her chirping barks would begin again in earnest.

After a couple of weeks of this failed nightly experiment, it became painfully clear she was not going to change. So, from mid-February on we adopted the routine of placing her in the bathroom each evening when we were ready for lights-out. Banishing her to that room filled me with guilt and regret as well, since our preference wasn't for her to spend full nights all by herself at this critical stage of her life. In the end, we simply had no choice but to do so, because we quite clearly couldn't go without sleep each night. Regardless, it's likely I always will feel badly that Codi didn't spend the last few weeks of her life sleeping in her customary spot at the side of our bed.

As the month of March came to a close, we were more concerned than ever that the BC finally was starting to feel some pain as a result of the cancer. What prompted that worry was a steadily increasing volume of the gurgling sound emanating from her abdomen after every meal, and the fact that incidents of loose stools were becoming far more frequent. The latter symptom was particularly concerning, because the inability to digest food properly was one of the signs of liver failure identified by the vet who had performed Codi's ultrasound test almost a year earlier. We just had to learn if she really was in pain. Based upon an earlier experience when she had major dental surgery, it was highly unlikely that *she* would ever directly let us know.

24. June 1999 – Major Dental Surgery

Codi's Frisbee obsession caused her to play with the toy in a manner that can only be described as reckless abandon. With a focus rivaling that of a professional athlete, she did whatever she had to do in order to catch that flying disk before it could hit the ground. Whenever she failed to grab it out of the air, you could see the frustration in her eyes as well as the determination not to miss the next throw. This resolve was so intense she even chose to catch tosses that were accidentally thrown directly at her head (as opposed to slightly over her head) at very high speed.

Each time I made such a throwing mistake, I yelled something to the effect of "No Codi, let it go," but the command always fell on deaf ears. I remember cringing all the time at the sound of the disk smacking her right in her open mouth. As intelligent as she was, she simply couldn't comprehend that it would be wiser to let it fly past her instead of catching the speeding bullet right in her chops. This wouldn't have been as much of a problem if we hadn't been using one of the hard-plastic Frisbees. The fact we were meant her teeth would occasionally experience some very significant trauma. Amazingly, though these experiences were undoubtedly quite painful for her, not one time did she ever show any indication of it by whining or crying.

By the time Codi was around four-years old, these shocks to her teeth, combined perhaps with some genetic factors, caused her to develop deep periodontal pockets around her upper and lower molars. At that time, our original vet treated this condition by inserting medicated cotton-like packs into the large gaps on the gum line. These would remain in for a few days, during which time a ball replaced the Frisbee as the toy of choice, since not giving her an opportunity to play (i.e., work) each day simply wasn't an option. The packs would ultimately dissolve or fall out, at which point we returned to playing with the flying disk.

These treatments continued on an annual basis until the spring of 1999 when Codi turned seven. At that time, I happened upon an article in the *Chicago Sun-Times* about a new trend toward the training of specialized *dental* veterinarians. The article went into great detail about the benefits of working with such specialists. It also included the name and number of one in Texas who was interviewed for the story. Given that the periodontal treatments Codi had been receiving were just a stopgap solution, I decided to contact that dental vet to see if there was a similar specialist working in the Chicago area. Fortunately there was. Her name was Dr. Barbara Stapleton, and her office was located in Barrington, about 40 minutes from our home.

Andrea and I agreed that taking Codi up there was a sound idea, so I promptly phoned the office and set up a morning appointment in mid-June 1999. On that day, we arrived at the scheduled time and I was informed the procedure would take perhaps two hours to complete. Naturally, it would be necessary to give her anesthesia. To better ensure her safety, she was also required to undergo blood testing to confirm that her liver was healthy enough to handle the anesthetic. This testing was conducted quickly and she passed with flying colors. The procedure began soon afterwards, and I decided to remain in the vet's waiting room rather than driving all the way home and returning later in the day.

Surprisingly, within less than 20 minutes, Dr. Stapleton came walking out of surgery to speak with me. When I saw her approaching, my heart began to race as my mind filled with fear that perhaps something really bad had happened to Codi. She quickly let me know the BC was just fine but, based on her initial, detailed exam, she concluded the procedure was going to take up to four hours to complete. She went on to explain that she had discovered a number of Codi's larger teeth had abscesses below the gum line while a handful of others (mostly incisors) were so loose they required extraction.

Dr. Stapleton recommended removing at least 12 teeth in total, including *all* of the upper and lower posterior teeth. Although I had a sense that many of Codi's teeth were in bad shape, I never figured it would be necessary to extract so many of them. I then asked if there was any other way to treat the problem. The answer was a swift no, as there was no alternative available that would ensure the infections could be halted in the surrounding tissues.

"How is she going to eat without those large molars," I asked. The vet replied that since dogs generally wolf down their food anyway, she'd still be able to eat without any problem. The days of chewing on milk bones and rawhide chews, however, would definitely be over for her. When I further inquired as to whether she'd be able to play Frisbee anymore, the answer fortunately, was yes, but with the added qualification that we'd need to switch to one of the newer, nylon fabric varieties. That was very encouraging news, given how much we both enjoyed playing with the flying disk each day.

The vet then excused herself to get back into surgery, while I settled in for a very long wait. The time was 11:00 a.m. I promptly phoned Andrea to fill her in on the situation and, naturally, she was very upset by the news. I assured her Codi was in very good hands and that I would keep her updated on things as soon as I heard anything more about the operation. I used the lengthy waiting time to work on my first book using a laptop I had brought along, though it was fairly challenging to make a whole lot of progress under the circumstances.

Time dragged as I found myself constantly looking up at the clock in the waiting room. Noon, 1:00, and 2:00 came and went before the vet finally returned at nearly 2:30 to fill me in on the results of the procedure. Her report was very positive as, despite having to tolerate over four hours of anesthesia, Codi currently was doing just fine in the recovery room. The bad news was that two additional teeth had to be extracted, bringing the total to 14, or exactly one-third of the 42 permanent teeth she originally had.

With respect to post-op care, the vet first mentioned they had given the BC some pain medication that would help to alleviate *some* of her discomfort over the next 24 hours. Dr. Stapleton then emphasized the importance of not allowing her to drink or eat too much that evening, as the extensive amount of anesthesia was likely to make her a bit nauseous. Given the major stress the surgery had placed on Codi's entire body, she also strongly suggested we keep her as quiet and subdued as possible. I assured the vet we'd be certain to follow those recommendations closely and thanked her heartily for her efforts. Prior to walking away, she added that Codi would be ready to leave within another half-hour or so. I then called Andrea and let her know the results of the procedure, and she was, of course, very relieved to hear that everything went well.

A little after three o'clock, a vet technician finally strolled into the waiting room with the BC walking slowly behind her. Once she spotted me, her tail began to wag back and forth very slowly and I immediately stepped forward to greet her with a hug and a soft kiss on the snout. I felt so relieved just to see her alive and well after so many hours under the anesthetic. My first impression was that other than looking exhausted she appeared to be in pretty good shape, particularly given the ordeal she had just undergone. Naturally, I felt very grateful that she had survived the complex procedure without issue but also felt deeply sorry for her having to suffer such a traumatic experience. Interestingly, while I was focused on the unfairness of what she was forced to endure that day, as usual Codi was fully centered in the present moment, as evidenced by her sharply yanking on the leash to let me know it was time to leave. She then turned and looked at me as if to say, "Can we *please* get out of this place?" Her message instantly registered with me. As a result, I quickly stepped forward to pay the rather hefty bill so we could finally get on the road.

During the entire trip home Codi was sound asleep, obviously exhausted from the surgery. I remember feeling very pleased that she was, in fact, resting instead of pushing herself, for it was obvious the day's events had taken a significant toll on her. When we finally arrived home nearly an hour later, both Andrea and Heidi were sitting on the front steps waiting for us. Surprisingly, Codi was so out of it that I had to wake her to let her know we had arrived back home. Once I did she slowly rose to her feet and began to wag her tail quite wildly as she realized exactly where she was.

A teary eyed Andrea opened the rear door of the car, picked her up, and then gave her a big hug. Codi squirmed to get down so she could respond to Heidi, who was jumping up and down and barking like crazy. Just like a happy ending in the movies, the family was together again and it felt absolutely wonderful! The dogs immediately took the opportunity to sniff each other in some detail, and then both of them walked towards the rear door of the garage that led out to the back yard. Despite still being a bit groggy from surgery and no doubt feeling substantial pain from having a third of her teeth removed, remarkably Codi actually bent down in an attempt to pick up her Frisbee! Fortunately, I was able to reach down and grab it prior to her reaching it and perhaps opening up one of the many stitches in her mouth.

I'll never forget that moment. Not only did it provide me with yet another demonstration of her renowned intensity, it also unmistakably indicated she was capable of handling an enormous amount of pain without ever showing any outward sign of it.

25. *Codi Speaks Again – April 1, 2005*

The nagging concern we had that Codi had begun to experience pain as a result of the cancer finally motivated me to arrange another session with Pam. The last time she met with her (nine weeks earlier), the BC indicated she preferred to leave on her own volition, but what if the illness had become so painful that she changed her mind about this?

We simply had to know where the condition stood in this regard, because just the thought of her seriously hurting deeply concerned us. Therefore, I made arrangements with Pam to meet with Codi again on Friday night April 1. As with the previous two sessions, the following *conversation* again represents a simplified version of the exchange of information that occurred between Pam and Codi that night:

Pam: Codi, your humans are very worried that your illness may have reached the point where you are now feeling some pain.

Codi: Yes, this is true. I am feeling pain but I'm still not ready to leave. I have some work to finish and, as I said to you once before, this is a path that I must walk. Tell them there is a lesson for them here, one of learning to accept what they cannot change and yet staying in a kind, loving, and patient place in spite of things.

Pam: That is a very difficult mental and emotional space for them to achieve, given how deeply they love you. Is there anything else you wish to tell either of them?

Codi: Yes, ask him to open his heart and the lessons that come will move him light years ahead in his growth. This journey for him is to learn the gentle acceptance of what is, not to think or to do but to *be*, with a heart fully open, accepting both the pain and the joy of looking into my eyes.

Pam: So is part of why you are remaining here because you need to teach him these lessons?

Codi: No, as I said this is my path to walk. It just so happens he is part of the circumstances but I didn't come into this life simply to teach him these lessons.

Pam: They want you to know they can't bear the thought of you being uncomfortable.

Codi: I understand how they both feel. Yes, as I said earlier, I am in pain but he, in particular, must understand this is *my* journey. He cannot control this.

Pam: Do you now wish for him to help you leave?

Codi: No, not at this moment. However, I *may* at some point ask for his assistance. Tell him *not* to ask me about it. I will make it very clear to him if and when the time comes that I need him to assist me.

Pam: He wants you to know that he still feels really badly about putting you in the bathroom each night at bedtime when you start barking.

Codi: I know they would both prefer that I remain with them. But tell them I'm fine with this solution because that little room gives me a sense of containment and helps me to feel calmer.

As with their first two visits, at this point Codi went silent, so Pam thanked her for the information and then ended the session.

26. April 1, 2005 – Meeting III Aftermath

During the post-session conversation, Pam emphasized that, although Codi's demeanor was very calm this time, she nonetheless was very forceful in what she said. Her sense was that the emphatic nature of the BC's communication was directly related to the fact that Codi now knew for certain she didn't have much time left. Her admission that she was finally experiencing some pain as a result of the cancer was, of course, not the news we wanted to hear. This, combined with the statement that she still didn't want us to help her leave, left us in a very uncomfortable predicament – either we help Codi leave against her wishes or we allow her to continue living in a state of potentially worsening pain.

We chose the latter and not the former because we trusted that the information Pam related to us from Codi was indeed accurate. In our hearts we felt she deserved the chance to finish the work she came to do. We just hoped she would do it quickly and leave on her own terms before the pain became much worse.

As in the previous two sessions, in addition to the information she shared about her pain status, Codi passed on some incredibly important "life advice" to us both. The point she raised once again about the need for us to be in *acceptance* of what *is*, even though at the very core of our beings we wanted to rebel against it, was very hard for us to put into practice. In reality, to us she was *our child*, and to see her dying right in front of our eyes and yet to be completely helpless to do anything to stop it was extremely frustrating. It was particularly challenging for me because, as I mentioned earlier in Chapter 14, my nature had always been to be a "make it happen" person, who carefully analyzed problems and then did whatever I could to solve them.

Codi's point about the extent to which I'd benefit by learning to *open my heart* was particularly relevant, given the historical affinity I had for living in my head. Interestingly, it mirrored exactly the advice my friend Lisa, had given me before on numerous occasions. Moreover, her guidance "not to think or to do, but to *be*" was likewise something very foreign to me, since one of my lifelong habits was, indeed, a fixation on *doing* as opposed to *being*. As with the earlier sessions with Pam, it once again was blatantly obvious that, somehow, *my dog* was keenly aware of critical life lessons *I* needed to learn.

When Pam relayed these words to me: "*accepting both the pain and the joy of looking into my eyes*," I remember immediately welling up with tears. The joy part was easy of course, the pain part clearly not so easy. Thinking back on what Codi communicated that day, difficult times like those demonstrate that *contrast* is what gives us the perspective needed to more deeply appreciate the good things we get to experience in life. Like the old cliché says, we must learn to take the bad with the good, for if there was no bad, we'd never know how good we actually have it. Yes, it was really terrible for Codi to have to endure this illness, and frustrating for us to be powerless to do anything to change it. But, our emotional anguish truly was a small burden to bear compared with the many years of tremendous joy and love that the BC had brought to us both.

With the knowledge that Codi was in pain now clearly in mind, and realizing she would, most likely, have only a few days left with us, our focus became even more riveted on making the most of the time that did remain.

27. Saturday, April 2 – Wednesday, April 6, 2005

The second day of April was a particularly important milestone because our beloved Codi was turning 13 years old. Miraculously, she had lived almost a full year with liver cancer, exceeding by several months the survival time estimated by the vet who originally diagnosed her. Although on the surface the current circumstances clearly left no reason for us to party, we nonetheless felt at least a muted celebration was in order to acknowledge the BC's ability to hang on for so long. We also made it a point that day to focus on how deeply grateful we were that she was still with us.

Back in late October, when there was some question as to whether Codi would be able to bounce back from that serious case of dehydration, I must admit neither of us honestly believed she'd make it to her next birthday. Once she was able to accomplish such an extraordinary recovery, however, I truly felt she would. In this regard, I still recall whispering the following in her ear on a regular basis, *"C'mon BC, you've got to make it 'til your 13th birthday. I know you can do it. Just hang on baby."* Even if it was just by a sliver, she sure did hang on and I was incredibly proud of her for doing so.

Sadly, because her digestive system could no longer handle any special dog treats, there wasn't much in the way of edible presents we could give her that day. So, in lieu of that, we made sure to give her a whole lot of attention. This we did with pleasure, of course, providing her with a few opportunities to fetch her squeaky toy throughout the day and evening and also making it a point to show her as much affection as she could handle. It was a good day indeed, but, as I was placing her in the bathroom at bedtime, I remember tearing up when the realization finally hit me – this would undoubtedly be the last birthday she would ever see.

Over the next few days Codi's condition steadily worsened, as evidenced by the louder and louder sounds emanating from her abdomen. There were also an increasing number of accidents inside the house; it had gotten to the point where these incidents would occur regardless of what we fed her. Because of this, we had to watch her very carefully for any signs of the onset of those symptoms. This way we could be in a position to quickly snatch her up and carry her outside. When we'd bring her back in after the episode had run its course, usually it was necessary to scrub her up a bit. While some might question why we didn't simply choose to protect the carpeting by keeping her isolated in the kitchen, the fact was we simply couldn't bring ourselves to insult the BC in this manner after 12 years of having free reign of the house.

Complicating the situation somewhat was my need to work outside of the home office on Tuesday through Thursday of that week. This, again, left the responsibility of caring for Codi squarely on Andrea's shoulders during the daytime. Given the BC essentially required constant monitoring, it would have made it a fairly stressful experience for anybody to deal with on their own. As expected though, Andrea handled the situation successfully with lots of love and compassion. The first two nights, I returned home from work to learn that Codi had made it through the days without any additional accidents. During both of those evenings, we continued to keep close watch over her and did our best to make sure she was as comfortable as reasonably possible under the circumstances. Not surprisingly, she remained very interested in playing, despite her pain and severely limited physical skills.

On Wednesday, the 6th, once again at bedtime I placed Codi and her dog bed in the bathroom for the night, turned on the nightlight, gave her some loving and headed off to bed. This particular night was different, however, in that her barking didn't trail off within a few minutes. She kept at it for quite some time. Eventually, I had no other choice but to close the door to our bedroom, as the sound of it was just too sad for us to handle.

Lying in bed that night, I was curious as to how much pain she was experiencing. I also felt desperate for her to somehow let me know if the time had finally come for us to help her leave. I wanted so badly to ask her. But at the same time, I simply wasn't willing to ignore her request (made through Pam) that I *not* do so. My decision was to wait a bit longer for some type of sign that she had definitely reached the point where she was ready for our assistance. Before dozing off to sleep, I said a prayer asking for guidance and wondered what the next day would bring.

28. *Thursday, April 7, 2005*

On this morning I left for my client's office somewhat earlier than usual because we had an extensive amount of work to finish during that final day. As I stated in a previous chapter, although I knew Codi would be in good hands with Andrea, I nevertheless felt really awful about leaving her again for an entire day. This particular day it was even more difficult to head out the door, given the extent to which her condition had deteriorated during the preceding few days. I hoped we'd be able to make enough progress on the project to enable me to get home sooner but wasn't very optimistic about the prospects.

Just after lunchtime I phoned Andrea to check in and learned that Codi had already been struck with a couple of bouts of diarrhea. Fortunately, she was able to get her outside for one of them but the other resulted in yet another mess on the carpet to clean up. Andrea added that Codi currently was napping, but during the morning she actually had enough energy to play with her favorite squeaky toy for several minutes. I thanked her for the call and asked her to be certain to phone me at once if things took a turn for the worse.

The rest of the afternoon I was so focused on finishing the project the hours just flew by. Before I knew it 6:00 came and went but, thankfully, we finally were wrapping things up. Andrea phoned at about half-past six to inquire as to when I was coming home, as she had to get to a volleyball match and didn't want to leave the BC alone. I told her I'd be home in less than 30 minutes so she could feel free to be on her way. She also reported that Codi was fast asleep in our bedroom and she didn't intend to disturb her. I was fine with that, figuring there was ample time for me to get home before something unfortunate might occur.

After hanging up the phone, I collected my few belongings and headed out to the car for the short drive home. Between the intense demands of the 11 hour workday and the emotional stress related to Codi's condition, I was totally exhausted and literally felt like I was in a daze. On the way, I suddenly remembered that for days I had wanted to stop by the Sears Auto Center to pick up a new motorcycle battery. So, I pulled into the Oakbrook Center mall and made my way over to the store.

Although it was dark by this time, the building was all lit up and very easy to see. I remember that while walking I was staring down at the asphalt, thinking about how I needed to complete this stop quickly in order to get home to Codi. Suddenly, as I swiftly strode toward what I thought was the handle of one of the entry doors, I instead smacked my head directly into the plate-glass window just to the right of the entrance.

At the moment of impact, a large thud rang out and everyone on the sales floor turned to look and see what the heck had happened. I stood there for a second or two, completely stunned as a severe pain throbbed in my nose. I then quickly stepped back from the window to collect myself. My first reaction was a feeling of utter embarrassment, followed promptly by a healthy dose of self-condemnation. Putting those feelings aside, I pulled one of the doors open and walked right up to the counter, where one of the salespeople promptly told me that the outside of my nose was bleeding quite profusely. I thanked her for letting me know, and then felt compelled to explain that I wasn't drunk or high, just extremely tired and distracted.

The salesperson suggested I go to the nearby men's room to get some paper towels to stem the bleeding, motioning toward where it was located. I replied that I already knew my way around the place very well because I had actually worked in that *same building* for three years during college! This fact alone made the whole experience even more surreal, for I had successfully walked through that particular store entrance two hundred times or more in the past.

Once in the restroom I looked in the mirror, where I saw a deep cut an inch or so down from the bridge of my nose. While I was able to slow the bleeding somewhat, I soon walked back to the sales floor to ask for (and luckily receive) a band-aid. With the wound successfully treated, I decided to put off my intended purchase and hurried home to take care of Codi.

Later that evening I relayed this bizarre story to my friend and healer/spiritual teacher, Lisa. She theorized that in the moment my face hit the window, from both a mental and emotional perspective, *I* wasn't even there. I couldn't help but agree with her supposition, because, in that instant, everything *but* my body was in fact focused elsewhere (i.e., on Codi). This experience powerfully demonstrated just how closely the BC and I were connected.

Fortunately, the Sears store was just three miles from our house so I was able to get home in less than five minutes. While pulling into the garage, I could see Heidi in one of the windows, barking like crazy. But Codi wasn't visible. This wasn't necessarily a bad sign since, over the preceding month or so, she essentially stopped looking out the window anyway. When I got in the house, Heidi greeted me at the back door in her typical enthusiastic manner. Still, there was no sign of Codi. In normal times this would be unheard of as both dogs always made their presence known as soon as either of us stepped foot in the house.

After calling her name a couple of times from the kitchen, my heart raced a bit. I ran toward the master bedroom where I found her lying motionless on her side. Her tail was perpendicular to her rear legs and behind her rear-end the carpet was stained. The poor pup obviously had another accident and didn't even have enough energy to stand up and move away from it. It was one of the saddest sights I'd ever seen in my life. The good news was that she was still alive and, as soon as I bent down near her head to say hello, her tail actually thumped a couple of times to acknowledge my arrival.

As she tilted her head up just a bit to look me in the eyes, I got the sense she was absolutely exhausted and also undoubtedly ashamed about this latest mishap. Reaching down, I gently grabbed her little head in my hands and told her not to be concerned, that everything was okay, and that I understood she would never have done this if she wasn't so sick. I then went into the kitchen to fetch the stain remover and other cleaning supplies.

When the clean-up task was completed, I lifted her up and carried her out the door and into the front yard to let her get some fresh air. Because she had significant intestinal issues that day and was, in all likelihood, dehydrated, later I decided to again use the turkey baster to give her some water. As usual, Codi cooperated fully with my efforts because she knew I was trying to help her.

As soon as she finished drinking, I decided it was time to talk to her very seriously about how dire the situation had become. I remember telling her I had done my best to respect her request not to ask if she wanted my help to leave. However, because her condition had worsened so dramatically, I just had to have some sign as to what she wanted me to do. With tears filling my eyes, I also told her that even though we would miss her terribly, this was simply no way for her to live anymore. Within just a couple of seconds after uttering those words, Codi walked slowly past me and onto the carpeting bordering the kitchen. She then turned around to face me, squatted down, and promptly had another episode.

I knew in my heart *this* was the sign I had asked her to give me, as she could just as easily have remained in the kitchen and done the exact same thing. Through this very deliberate act, I felt Codi had, indeed, made it perfectly clear it was time for me to help her leave. As she walked away from this latest mess and directly toward me, I knelt down and hugged her, then whispered softly in her ear that I understood *exactly* what she was trying to tell me.

Like it or not, it was finally time to let her go. In that moment, the decision was made. I felt as if a large weight had been lifted from my shoulders. If you, too, have faced the difficult choice to put a pet down, then my sense is you can really relate to what I'm saying. The reality is, when we make any major life decision there is always a feeling of relief, because we're finally able to leave the paralysis of indecision behind. While we might not at all like the ultimate consequence of what we decided, we're better for having made it since at least we're moving forward again in some way. Pulling back from holding her close, I told her I would make arrangements for us to visit the animal hospital on Saturday morning, for that was when Dr. Laura Clarke would be working next. With all the kindness and compassion Laura had extended to our family the past few years, I couldn't imagine any other vet performing that procedure for us.

The next half-hour or so I spent in my office listening to voice mails, and catching up on e-mails. To make certain I was able to keep an eye on Codi at all times, I placed her dog bed and her on the floor a couple of feet behind my chair. She slept soundly in that place until Andrea arrived home, at which point she was awakened by Heidi's enthusiastic barking. When Andrea walked into the office Codi pulled her head up to get a look at her and also wagged her tail a few times.

After stooping down to pet her, she inquired as to how she was doing. In the process of updating her on all that had happened, it didn't take long for Andrea to start crying and for me to follow suit. As we stood there hanging on to each other for a spell, the sadness just poured out of us in waves. Although we intellectually knew there might well come a day when we'd have to make that fateful decision about euthanasia, from an emotional standpoint we obviously had chosen to suppress the terror we felt about ever having to do so.

In the midst of our embrace, we heard Codi trying to push herself up onto her feet. So, we quickly separated and I bent down to help her. Once steady, she walked slowly to the kitchen and lapped up quite a bit of water. This was definitely a positive sign, given how lifeless she had appeared throughout the course of the evening. I then decided to be a bit proactive by letting her outside again, just in case she felt another urge to go.

When I returned to the office to wrap things up for the night, much to my surprise the BC promptly walked in carrying her squeaky toy. I remember initially being a bit shocked to see this, following the difficult day she just had. After a moment or two, however, it made great sense to me, given how intensely dedicated she had always been to her work. (Please refer to a photo near the end of the photo gallery to see how Codi looked during this final stage of her life.) It only took a handful of tosses to tire her out but I cannot express to you how inspiring it was to see her playing that night. Despite being in pain and having severely limited physical skills, she *willed* herself to do something she absolutely loved to do. In the process of doing so, she again set a powerful example for us to emulate in our own lives.

As bedtime arrived that evening, we once more placed her in the bathroom she had adopted as her den during the past two months. Andrea and I each took turns stroking her and telling her just how much we loved her before closing the door and heading off to bed. Falling asleep that night took longer than usual, as my mind was whirring with thoughts about the arrangements that needed to be made the following day.

29. *Friday, April 8, 2005*

As this day began, my initial order of business was to go check on Codi in the bathroom. The good news was she was somewhat perky, despite the tough time she had the previous day. It also was encouraging to find she didn't have an accident overnight. After I let both dogs out to do their business, Andrea took over the responsibility of keeping a close watch on the BC. I headed into my office to start working on the plans for Saturday. Looking back, it's now obvious that focusing on the business aspects of the situation gave me an opportunity to distract myself briefly from thinking about what was to occur the next day.

My first step was to call Dr. Clarke at home to update her about the events of the preceding days, and to tell her about our intention to visit the animal hospital the following morning. When Laura answered the phone, she didn't sound surprised to hear from me and was, of course, very sad to learn the time had finally come for Codi to leave us. She readily agreed to call the hospital receptionist on my behalf to arrange a time for us. Because of the driving distance involved, I asked if we also could reserve some time for Heidi's annual check-up. A few minutes later she called back to let me know an appointment for both dogs had been confirmed for 11:00 a.m.

The next step was to make a decision regarding the handling of Codi's remains once the medical procedure was completed. In my heart, I preferred to bury her right in our yard but when I thought carefully about how hard it would be for me to actually *do* so, I knew cremation was the only option that made sense for us. The simplest approach would have been to ask the animal hospital to deal with the details. However, I chose to handle it myself because I wanted to be certain the ashes we ultimately received were actually Codi's. This is not to suggest the animal hospital would deliberately allow the opposite to occur, but the truth is they contract the service to a third-party vendor over which they have no control. Since, in the past, I had heard negative stories about cremation service providers doing mass cremations of deceased animals, I simply had to work directly with whoever would take care of Codi's remains.

To find potential providers, I used the yellow pages and quickly came across an advertisement placed by the Hinsdale Animal Cemetery, located just a few miles from our house. I phoned to ask for details regarding their services, and was connected promptly to a very friendly and compassionate man. In response to my desire for some assurance regarding the receipt of *only* Codi's ashes after the cremation, he informed me about an extra-cost service guaranteeing this would occur. Following a brief conversation in which he dutifully answered all of my other questions, I made an appointment for the next afternoon.

What most inspired me to use their services was an offer permitting me to actually attend the procedure at the scheduled time. And, I could do so without giving them any notice whatsoever. While I couldn't imagine really doing that, I was nonetheless impressed by their commitment to the integrity of the process. With the necessary arrangements completed, the rest of the day was dedicated to spending quality time with Codi.

Walking into our bedroom, where Andrea was sitting with both dogs nearby, I knelt down to pet the BC and Heidi quickly interrupted me to get some attention for herself. Over the course of their lives together, this was quite common. Whenever one of them was getting stroked the other *always* showed up to demand similar consideration. It was a friendly rivalry though, and I truly got the sense that they really came to care about one another very deeply. The competition between them was, most likely, a natural offshoot of their pack mentality. Even though Heidi had long ago acknowledged Codi's position as the alpha dog, she still couldn't resist challenging her now and then. And, from the BC's perspective, she knew that occasionally she'd have to put Heidi in her place and didn't ever shy away from doing so. Because of their close connection, I couldn't help but wonder how Heidi would handle Codi's departure from the pack.

Sitting on the bedroom floor that afternoon, I noticed again quite clearly the loud gurgling sounds coming from Codi's abdomen. While there obviously was no way of knowing exactly what was happening inside her, my sense was that the cancer had become so advanced it had finally wrapped itself completely around her digestive organs. I was totally certain she was experiencing tremendous pain at this stage and yet, once again, her will to live was clearly exhibited by the interest she showed in playing with her squeaky toy.

Watching her walk slowly back and forth to retrieve the toy was particularly heart-wrenching on this, her last full day. It brought back memories of better times when she could run like a blue streak and leap sky high to pluck her Frisbee out of the air. 'Where had the time gone,' I recall musing, for it seemed like it was just yesterday when we brought her home for the first time. Seemingly in the wink of an eye 13 years had elapsed and now we found ourselves less than 24 hours away from the moment we'd have to say goodbye forever to our beloved friend. The plain truth was, the whole situation *sucked*, but remaining in that frame of mind the rest of the day and night wouldn't have been fair to Codi. Therefore, I made a conscious effort to shift out of such thoughts, instead focusing on giving as much loving attention to her as possible.

Despite having at least a moderate appetite earlier in the day, at the evening feeding time Codi made it very clear she wasn't interested in eating anything. Given the circumstances, it made absolutely no sense to spend any time trying to convince her to eat, so we just let her *be*. The rest of the night she lay peacefully on her dog bed in the bedroom, and every few minutes Andrea and I would kneel down to check on her and give her some loving.

Just prior to bedtime, I carried Codi out in the front yard with Heidi following along to do her business as well. I again stood next to the BC steadying her while she struggled even more than usual with the task. Regrettably, she again was plagued by a serious bout of intestinal discomfort. I had hoped she'd get through her final night without having to deal with any more of that infirmity because doing so really wore her out. It was kind of surprising she did have another episode of it, given she hadn't really eaten very much at all that day.

With both dogs back in the house and settled in, Andrea and I set about getting ready for sleep. When the time actually came to get into bed, no matter how much I dreaded having to put Codi in the bathroom on the last night she'd ever be with us, I knew in my heart it was best. She had become so accustomed to being in her sleeping "den," it just intuitively made sense to stick with that routine. Even so, I still find myself wishing this hadn't been the case. Both Andrea and I would have absolutely loved to have the BC spend her final night with us in her customary position at the side of our bed.

Before putting her in there, Andrea and I knelt down on the bedroom floor with her and did a brief "group hug" that included Heidi as well. After some heavy sobbing on both our parts, I lifted Codi up and carried her off with Andrea following directly behind with the dog bed. Once we got her settled in the bathroom we hugged her another time, told her again how much we loved her and how grateful we were for her presence in our lives.

Gazing into her eyes that night, I just *knew* she understood everything we were saying. I also got the sense she knew her mission was now complete, that she had walked the full length of the path she had chosen for this life. All that remained was to leave behind her cancer-ridden and very painful body, and it was now up to us to assist her with this final step. After turning on the nightlight, I looked intensely into her eyes one last time, and then softly whispered in her ear that the pain would soon end. Closing the door behind me I headed off to bed, where I quietly shed a few more tears before finally succumbing to sleep.

30. *Saturday, April 9, 2005*

When we look back upon our lives, it's very rare for us to have anywhere near perfect recall of even a portion of any particular day we've lived. The truth is, our days tend to blend together and only in exceptional instances does one day stand apart from any other. Examples of unusual occasions where we are inclined to have more detailed recollections include, most notably: a wedding day, the birth of a child, and the loss of a loved one.

In my life there have been only a handful of those days, and, until the moment my soul chooses to depart this earth, I *know* that Saturday, April 9, 2005, always will be one of them. As I awakened that morning, I remember thinking, 'God I hope Codi decided to leave on her own overnight…I just can't bear the thought of watching her die.' Approaching the bathroom door, I must admit having a strong desire to find a lifeless body in there so I didn't have to endure that experience. However, this was not the manner in which her life would end.

As the door slowly swung open, I was greeted by a very heart rending sight. Codi had experienced a major accident and soiled a big portion of her dog bed. Worse yet, because of her weakened state she again wasn't able to get up and distance herself at all from the effects of it. Hearing the doorknob turn, she gradually lifted her head to look at me, and, as our eyes met, I found myself overwhelmed with sorrow on her behalf. I likewise felt somewhat guilty for not having checked on her sooner.

I immediately called out to Andrea to fill her in on

what had occurred and asked her to start running water in the other bathtub. There was no way I was going to have Codi experience further humiliation by taking her to the vet's office with any remnant of the accident on her coat. Carefully sidestepping the mess, I gently picked the BC up and carried her into the other bathroom to wash her. Whereas in the past she would be struggling quite aggressively to avoid a trip into the tub, this time she was completely docile. She simply didn't have any energy left to protest.

After a mild but thorough scrubbing, I dried Codi and then took her into the front yard to see if she needed to go. As I had done other times when she was particularly weak, I used a towel underneath her belly to steady her. Within seconds of her paws hitting the ground she squatted and immediately had intestinal problems again. To help ensure that she got everything out of her system, I kept her outside for a few more minutes. Once back in the house we ran bathwater and then washed and dried her a second time.

When Codi was finally ready to transport, I carried her out to the car where Andrea and Heidi were already waiting in the backseat. Because of the potential for another flare-up, Andrea had placed an old comforter on her lap and also brought along an old bath towel in case Codi did lose control of her bowels again. I distinctly remember that, as I lowered the BC onto Andrea's lap, her body felt almost lifeless and her eyes had a dazed look, making her appear as if she was barely conscious. In that moment, we wondered if she would even live through the 45-minute trip to the vet's office. Driving down the interstate, I regularly looked in the rearview mirror to check on how things were going in the backseat. Andrea kept stroking Codi tenderly the entire time, while simultaneously paying enough attention to Heidi to ensure she remained somewhat calm during the long drive.

Following what seemed to be an eternity, we arrived at the hospital, at which point we decided the best approach was to first have Dr. Clarke (i.e., Laura) take care of Heidi's annual check-up. Prior to exiting the car, I reached back to pat the BC on the head and was very touched at the site of her lying so peacefully on her *mommy's* lap, just as she had done during that first drive home with her as a 10-week old puppy. Codi's life had obviously come full circle, and soon all that would be left of this nearly 13 year experience would be photographs, videos, and memories. Knowing full well my close connection with the BC, Andrea kindly asked if I would prefer changing places with her. I declined, thinking it was best to leave Codi undisturbed until it was absolutely necessary to move her. I then attached Heidi's leash and led her out of the car and into the vet's office.

Laura emerged a short time later to warmly greet us both and promptly escorted us to an examining room. On the way I let her know that Andrea was waiting in the car with Codi. She asked if I wanted to go ahead and bring the BC in as well. I answered "no," since I remember my friend, Lisa, had warned me to keep Heidi out of the room when Codi passes on, because the experience could cause her to be terrified of future visits to the vet. Once settled in the room, Laura asked how we were holding up under the circumstances. I replied that, overall, we were doing okay with things because it was now agonizingly clear Codi needed to be put down in order to prevent further suffering. Laura then sympathetically reached out and gave me a big hug, and she also took a moment to acknowledge us for the excellent care we gave the BC over the course of her illness. Holding on to her tightly, I thanked her for her kindness and told her how deeply we appreciated all she personally had done for us during the preceding six months.

Heidi's exam was completed in about 20 minutes, Laura pleased to report at its conclusion that "the little pup" (our nickname for her) appeared to be in virtually perfect health for her age of nearly 10 years. Given what we'd been through with Codi in the past year, it was very relieving to hear such good news about Heidi's fitness.

With that exam finished, the time had finally come to face the event we had been dreading. As you may already know, it is one thing to talk about putting a pet down, but it's an entirely different thing to actually be present in the room when it occurs. I knew this all too well from personal experience. Back in December 1995 my brother and I had to take my mom's 11 year-old dog, Heidi, in for the same procedure. I will *always* remember that day as well because it was I who gently held her down while the vet inserted the needle into her front leg. Watching the animating energy leave her body was truly a life-changing experience. By no means did I want to go through the same thing again. And yet, no matter how hard it would be to stay in the room when Laura administered euthanasia, choosing to avoid the experience would have been extremely unfair to Codi. Given how deeply connected we had been for so many years, there was no way I could justify *not* being with her at the moment of her passing.

As Heidi and I prepared to leave the examining room, Laura inquired as to where our car was parked. I stated that it was right in front of the hospital entrance. She then suggested that given the severity of Codi's condition, it might be better for us to avoid the stress of bringing her in through the crowded waiting room. Instead she suggested we use a rear entrance door. I fully agreed and proceeded outside to get Heidi back into the car and then to move it to the parking lot at the back of the facility.

When we entered the car, Andrea's face had an obvious look of relief at seeing us finally return. She said Codi was still alive but just barely. Her respiration rate had dropped significantly and her eyes were showing very little movement. I reached back to stroke her head and her eyes opened slightly to acknowledge me. Once the car was moved, I cracked a couple of windows to make sure Heidi had fresh air while we were inside the hospital. After reassuring the little pup we'd return shortly, I opened the driver's side rear car door, reached down to pick up the BC from Andrea's lap and the three of us then headed toward the rear door of the hospital.

Holding Codi to my chest with her head resting on my left shoulder, I distinctly remember feeling incredibly guilty in one sense to be carrying my best friend off to her death. At the same time, however, the fact she was barely conscious and essentially lifeless as we entered the examining room completely confirmed the appropriateness of what was to occur. Laura, who hadn't seen the BC since late October, obviously was visibly shaken by just how dramatically her body had deteriorated. Checking her heart rate, she reported that it was so slow it wouldn't even be necessary to inject her with a sedative normally used for calming.

Laura then asked if we would like a few minutes alone with Codi prior to her delivering the injection. Since Andrea and I were very distraught by this time and not thinking very clearly, we decided to proceed immediately without any additional holdup. Thinking back to that moment, this is a decision I still have some regret about. What serves to temper my remorse, however, is my knowing the BC was in tremendous pain at that point and every additional second we delayed would have merely amplified it.

With that choice made, Laura asked us both to stand next to Codi's head and stroke her gently while she inserted the needle containing the fatal medication in one of her rear legs. Sobbing intensely, we bent down to draw within a few inches of her snout, looked deeply into her eyes and told her again just how much we loved her and appreciated her being a part of our family. Although nearly unconscious, she looked up at us with her beautiful brown eyes for one final time. In a matter of less than 10 seconds, her gaze went blank and her body became limp.

Just like that, she was gone. Staring down at her lifeless, cancer-ravaged body I again wondered where all the time had gone. Nearly thirteen years had disappeared as if in a flash of light, and now all that was left was the outer shell of a beloved companion who always loved us unconditionally and who gave us immeasurable joy as well. In that final moment, Andrea and I instinctively drew together in crying gasps, hugging each other intensely and trembling with sorrow. Laura's eyes had also welled up with tears and she approached us to join in our embrace. The three of us stood there holding each other close for perhaps half a minute until the vet tech inadvertently made a noise that startled us out of our reverie.

Laura then proceeded to gently wrap Codi in the old comforter she had been lying on in the car. As we watched her doing so, we again felt deeply grateful to have been fortunate enough to connect with such a compassionate veterinarian. Perhaps the fact that she had three dogs of her own was the foundation for her empathy, but my sense was it was only a part of it. The truth is she quite simply loves animals so much that she treats each one with the same respect and kindness she would give to her own.

With the BC's body safely wrapped for transport, it was finally time for us to leave. I reached down to the examining table and picked up the comforter and both of us followed Laura to the back door, where she hugged each of us one last time. We both thanked her profusely, and then made our way out to the car where Heidi was waiting anxiously for us to return. As I placed Codi's remains in the trunk, Andrea quickly got in the car and gave some attention to Heidi who had begun barking and squealing with delight.

As I climbed into the driver's seat, the little pup's

attention shifted from Andrea to me and I was enthusiastically greeted with lots of licks. In addition, several times during the ride home she put her two front feet on the console and leaned over to each of us to give us some additional kisses. After what we had just been through, it felt absolutely wonderful to receive so much loving from our remaining pup. To me, it was obvious that, at some level, she *knew* what had occurred. In response, she was doing her best to comfort us with as much affection as she could muster.

Despite these very welcomed efforts on Heidi's part to break through the energy of sadness in the car, both of us continued to battle our grief throughout the ride home. The fact was, even though we knew what was going to happen, we still were very traumatized by the experience itself. While we both would have preferred to just go home and crash on the couch for the rest of the day, there was one final place we obviously needed to visit that afternoon – the animal cemetery.

Before heading over to the cemetery, we decided it was best to drop Heidi off at home so she could eat her midday meal. We also concluded it wasn't appropriate to take her with us as we had no idea how long it would take to complete the arrangements. While the thought of allowing Heidi the opportunity to see and sniff Codi one last time did cross my mind, in the end we opted not to do so because we thought it might just upset her in some way.

After saying goodbye to the little pup, we took off

for the short drive to the cemetery. Pulling away from the house, it occurred to us that, over the course of her life, there were just a few times when she had been left completely alone. Being a pack animal, she'd most likely feel some level of anxiety as a result. We hoped she wouldn't be overly stressed but we also knew that from now on this clearly was something she'd have to get accustomed to.

The animal cemetery was a fairly crowded place that day. In addition to people interested in cremation services, the conventional burial ground for pets had numerous visitors. We walked in to the visitor center and asked to see the gentleman who had made the initial arrangements with me over the phone. He entered the lobby and greeted us warmly, expressed his condolences in a very sincere manner, then immediately asked us where we were parked so he could have someone retrieve Codi's remains.

After I replied, he posed another question that totally surprised us: "Would you like us to place Codi in a private viewing area so you can have a few minutes to say goodbye to her a final time?" When Dr. Clarke had wrapped the BC tightly in the comforter, the truth was we both felt this would be the last time we'd actually see her. We hadn't even considered the possibility of another occasion to say goodbye because we thought it might cause us to relive the difficult moment of her passing. Nonetheless, after just a moment of hesitation, something inspired me to say yes. Andrea quickly nodded in agreement.

As we waited in the office for a staff member to retrieve Codi's remains from the car, we took the opportunity to select a wooden photo box for her ashes and to settle up the financial aspect of the arrangements. With that complete, we were led to the small room where her body awaited us. Our first step into the space was a bit unnerving, but as soon as we saw her lying on a small bier, we both knew we had made the right choice. Because things had moved so swiftly at the animal hospital, we didn't have the time to just *be* with her for a few minutes following her passing. There's no doubt that having the opportunity to stand there gazing at our beloved pup in such a tranquil setting was a very healing experience for us both.

I recall staying in that room for several minutes, during which time we shared a number of "do you remember when?" type tales about some of the more memorable moments in her life. For example, we giggled a bit while reminiscing about some of her more comical behaviors, including those episodes early in her life when she'd go "Border Collie Crazy" throughout the house. We also chuckled about that time the Golden Lab puppy bounded into the street and frightened Codi to the point that she actually tried to leap into my arms. We likewise recalled the times when we'd purposely squeak her toy in rapid succession and, in response, she'd rapidly bounce her front legs up and down as if she were dancing.

In addition to calling to mind such amusing past experiences, having this extra time with her allowed us to more fully express our remorse at her passing. The emotions flowed quite steadily that afternoon as we stared down at what little remained of Codi's formerly powerful physical form. Over the course of her final year, her weight had literally dropped in half from 40 pounds to just 20. Yet right up until the day before she passed, Codi never lost her intense will to live. This commitment on her part to live life to the fullest evoked within us a deep feeling of respect and admiration that we'll never forget. Though beleaguered by grief that afternoon, we also talked about how incredibly blessed we felt to have had the opportunity to share nearly 13 years of our lives with such an amazing being.

Prior to leaving the room, we both bent down and gave Codi a final pet and a kiss on the snout. Wiping my eyes as I stepped away from her body, the idea suddenly occurred to me to take a lock of her hair with us. While I thought scissors might be perceived as an odd thing to ask for, we quickly learned it was actually a very common request. Within just a minute or so of asking for them a pair was brought in. Looking down at Codi, my eyes were instantly drawn towards the very tip of her tail with its Border Collie trademark white-colored fur. This was the ideal place from which to gather the lock, since the strands of hair were quite lengthy in that area. I carefully clipped off about four inches and placed it in an envelope that the office staff was kind enough to give me.

With that memento safely in hand, we left the room, stopping one last time at the door for a final look at our dear friend. From there, we went by the office again to express our gratitude for all their support and kindness, and were told we would receive a phone call once Codi's ashes were ready for pickup. We also were informed of the scheduled day and time of the cremation, just in case we wanted to be there. Attending that event, however, was not something we had any interest in at all. Based on how kindly we were treated, there was not a doubt in our minds they would treat Codi with immense respect and provide the exact service that had been promised.

During the drive home, we both felt very physically and emotionally spent by the day's events. In a way, I suppose it was kind of like being in a state of shock where one just feels numbed by all the pain. There was little conversation between us because there simply wasn't much else to say about the circumstances that hadn't already been said. An era had indeed passed and we now, quite obviously, had to begin a new period of our lives.

When we reached the house and pulled into the driveway we immediately saw Heidi jump up into the window with her ears back and yelping with joy. Talk about a sight for sore eyes. Just then our mood shifted from despair to delight as we climbed out of the car and raced into the house to see her. While I worked to unlock the back door, we instantly heard the familiar sound of Heidi's nails scraping against it in her zeal to welcome us.

As we knelt down to greet her, both of us were attacked immediately with dog kisses and repeated squeals of happiness. Oh what a tremendous feeling it was to soak up all of that unconditional canine love after such a demanding day! Looking back, I cannot imagine how much more difficult it would have been for us to recover from the heartbreak of watching Codi die if Heidi hadn't been a part of our family that day. The loving attention she gave us the balance of that Saturday helped to ease the pain associated with such a horrendous loss.

Early that evening, we took the little pup for a walk around the neighborhood. This was something we hadn't been able to do with her for several months, out of deference to Codi. While it seemed a bit odd to be walking as a group of three, as opposed to four, in another sense it felt good to be outside enjoying the fresh air again, considering we had been house-bound for so long. At certain moments during our stroll, I honestly got the feeling Codi's spirit was there with us. After all, it was a course we had taken perhaps hundreds of times as a foursome over the preceding nine years. Initially, Heidi appeared a bit disoriented, probably because the BC as the alpha dog was no longer there to take the lead role. By the time we were a few blocks from home, however, it was obvious she had gained the confidence to assume her new leadership position.

Later that night after dinner, Andrea and I settled down to watch a video on our double-reclining loveseat. Exhausted from the stress of the day's events, it wasn't long before we dozed off, only to be startled awake by Heidi as she jumped up, wedged her way in between us and curled up in a tight little ball. Perhaps she once again knew we needed some puppy love, or maybe she felt lonesome herself without her pal there anymore to keep her company. Possibly it was a bit of both.

Whatever the reason, it didn't matter to us. We were just delighted to have her so close to us. The little pup also comforted us by sleeping at the end of the bed that night, snuggled tightly between our legs. Lying there just before falling asleep, I remember thinking how strange it was to no longer have to be concerned about the BC's welfare. While in one sense it was a relief, the more dominant feeling was one of sadness at the void that resulted from her departure. The following paraphrased quotation from the movie, "The Shawshank Redemption," best captures how I felt at the time:

"It makes me sad though, Codi being gone.

I have to remind myself that beings like her don't belong trapped in a diseased body. Their spirit is just too vibrant, and when they pass on, the part of you that knows it was a sin to want them to stay does rejoice, but still the place you live in is just that much more drab and empty that they are gone…I guess I just miss my friend."

Codi finally had passed on and left behind her suffering. All that remained for us to do was to pick up her ashes the following week and, afterwards, to identify an appropriate way to honor her for all the love and enjoyment she brought to us over the years.

31. *Closure*

In the week immediately following Codi's passing, Heidi played an invaluable role in comforting us and in distracting us from our heartache. Her presence likewise helped to ease our transition away from the role of essentially serving as hospice care providers for the better part of the preceding six months. As a home-based writer, I was particularly impacted by this shift in focus, since monitoring the BC's welfare and whereabouts within the house had commanded quite a bit of my attention during that time. Fortunately, in addition to having Heidi to divert my attention, there was quite a bit of technical writing work to keep my mind occupied during the first week without her.

Despite these diversions, feelings of sorrow would occasionally overcome me as my mind relived memories of various experiences Codi and I shared over the years. I distinctly recall remarking one day to my friend, Lisa, that without the BC around it felt as if there was "a hole in my heart." If you've lost a beloved animal companion, I'm sure you know precisely what I mean. When people say a pet is "*like* a member of the family," I actually have to differ. In my experience, they *are* a member of the family in every sense of the term. As odd, or perhaps controversial as this may sound, losing Codi was, *conceptually,* every bit as difficult for me as the loss of a child would have been to a parent.

About five days after Codi died, we received a voice message from the animal cemetery letting us know her ashes and photo box were ready for pickup. That day I was working at my client's site so Andrea took the responsibility for collecting them. She phoned me at the office late in the day to advise me she had completed the task and was on her way home. She also mentioned the ashes were sealed in a cardboard container, adding that she would wait for me to return so we could open it together. The remainder of the afternoon I found it a bit difficult to concentrate. I was pretty anxious to get home and open the package.

When I finally arrived Andrea let Heidi out in the front yard, where she greeted me in her usual enthusiastic way (i.e., lots of kisses and squealing barks). I reveled in the positive energy she so willingly shared with me and gave her plenty of attention in return. After a few tosses of her tennis ball, we both headed inside to settle in for the evening. While Heidi was busy eating her evening meal, Andrea and I walked into my office to open the package. We were very pleased to find the container was, in fact, the exact style and color we requested. We stood there for about a minute holding it in our hands, during which time both of us began to cry a bit. With Codi's ashes now home, the final chapter of the story of her life with us indeed had reached its closure.

The only thing left for us to do was to find an appropriate photo of the BC and place it in the picture slot. I promptly set about that task, rummaging through numerous photo albums in an attempt to locate some alternatives that captured both her beauty and intensity. Although there were several good options, we ultimately agreed on a very captivating picture of her taken while she was sitting on our bed. We placed the photo box on top of a shelving unit in my office that already included some photos

of Codi, as well as a beautiful illustration of her that my
sister-in-law Roseann had drawn for us as a present more
than a decade earlier.

Some weeks later, Andrea presented me with a very
special gift – a beautiful custom picture frame consist-
ing of a series of photos from various times in Codi's life
and surrounding a larger picture of the BC and me. It was
added to what we eventually came to call the Codi shrine
– the manner in which we chose to honor her. Though,
initially, just looking at this memorial tended to evoke
deep-seated feelings of sadness within us both, over time
it's become something we cherish as a reminder of all of the
wonderful times we spent with the BC over the years. The
process of getting to this point, however, required us to
progress through quite a lengthy grieving period.

32. *Grieving*

The first few weeks following Codi's passing flew by as we busied ourselves catching up on activities put aside during the last few months of her life. Though this busyness helped to divert our attention from the pain, we nevertheless continued to grieve her loss very deeply. It was in the quiet moments that memories of her would return to remind us of how much we missed her. Thankfully, Heidi continued to do a tremendous job of distracting us from our sadness but it just wasn't possible for her to completely fill the paws which had departed.

At some level, I suppose we felt like the BC was still with us. Maybe this was the underlying reason why I laundered her dog bed a couple of days after she died, then left it at the foot of our bed for a spell. If nothing else, I thought perhaps Heidi could put it to good use. Interestingly though, our feeling about Codi's continued presence in *some* form seemed to be supported by Heidi's conduct with respect to the dog bed – she wouldn't lay down or step a foot on it a single time. Moreover, whenever she'd walk directly toward it, just prior to placing a paw down to touch it she would pause for a second then turn and completely *walk around it.*

That behavior so captivated us that I phoned Pam, the animal communicator, and left a message about it. When returning my call, she said it was certainly possible Codi's spirit was making an appearance. And Heidi, sensing her energy, instinctively followed the previously established pack protocol by staying off her bed. The fact that Heidi never laid on the dog bed when the BC was alive suggested to us that Pam's explanation was certainly plausible. While it's also possible Heidi avoided the bed because it still contained the BC's scent, this alone couldn't explain why she chose not to even set foot on it. Although we couldn't actually *feel* Codi's presence, the mere thought that her spirit might be around the house was very comforting to us.

Something by no means reassuring to me, was a nightmare about Codi's passing that I experienced on two different occasions a couple of months after she was gone. In each instance, I saw myself carrying her up the rear steps of the animal hospital on the day she was euthanized. The visual aspects of the dream were very accurate with respect to the details of that actual experience and were accompanied by a stern voice at the end saying, "How *could* you have taken your own best friend off to her death?" Both times I was startled awake by that voice and then quickly sat up in bed, feeling very disturbed. Even though I *knew* putting her down that day was completely necessary, this nightmare illustrated that, at a subconscious level, I obviously felt some serious remorse for actually having done it.

A few days after the dream occurred the second time, I had an opportunity to speak with my friend and acupuncturist, John Honey, about it. I had gone to see him for some treatment and, at the close of the session I filled him in about the details of the nightmare. Just as I finished doing so, I felt a wave of emotion flow over me and my eyes immediately welled up. Just then I reached out, grabbed

John in a bear-hug, and out of nowhere, these words blurted out of me: "Johnny I feel so badly about carrying my poor pup to her death. I feel like I killed her myself." John, who is one of the most eccentric and metaphysically oriented people I've ever met, held on to me tightly and instantly replied, "Incoming transmission from the Universe – Codi wants you to know she would have done the same for you if the circumstances were reversed."

As soon as those words reached my ears, a big smile came over my face and I actually started to giggle a bit. I gave John another big squeeze and thanked him for such an inspiring and timely insight. Having known him for several years, I was certain he didn't make that statement flippantly. And, because he replied so quickly I felt in that moment he really did say *her* words and not his own. Those without a metaphysical slant would argue against this, but if Pam could somehow communicate with Codi's spirit, then it was certainly *possible* John could as well. Whatever the source of the information, there was no doubt it provided me with great comfort. Best of all, after that visit with John I never experienced the same nightmare again.

Before we knew it the trees had lost their leaves, Christmas 2005 had come and gone and the one-year anniversary of Codi's death in April 2006 was behind us as well. While time hadn't really "healed the wound," the business of day-to-day life steadily diverted enough of our attention during the preceding 11 months to at least allow it to scab up a bit. That didn't mean we no longer thought about Codi. The reality was not a day went by when an image of her failed to cross either of our minds. Seemingly, we had just reached the place of full acceptance of her passing and also *appeared* to have moved beyond the point of experiencing deep emotional pain as a result of it.

As the old saying goes, however, appearances can be deceiving. This became abundantly clear during August of 2006 while Andrea and I were on vacation in Ireland. After two very enjoyable days in Dublin, we embarked upon an extended drive through the rolling hills of the Irish countryside. In preparation for the trip I had packed some CDs to listen to on my portable player and, just by chance, the rental car included a CD player. One afternoon on our way from the Rock of Cashel to Kilkenny, I popped in a wonderful recording called the *End of the Innocence* by Don Henley, turned up the volume, and we both sang along with all of the tunes. By the time we got to the next to the last song on the CD, Andrea and I both were singing in full voice and having a grand ole' time.

As the final cut on the CD called "The Heart of the Matter" began, we continued our choral efforts until the song reached this line: *"I'm learning to live without you now, but I miss you sometimes."* Once I sang those words, tears began pouring down my face as pictures of Codi at various stages of her life suddenly flashed through my mind. Andrea immediately noticed my singing had stopped, and also saw the water rolling down my cheeks. She quickly reached over to grab my hand and comfort me. In doing so she got a bit weepy as well. I was so filled with gloom in those moments I considered pulling off on the side of the road to compose myself. Fortunately, that step wasn't necessary but it did take me a few minutes to calm down. I guess, in some sense, Andrea and I both were surprised that, nearly 16 months after Codi passed, we still could be struck by such intense feelings of sadness.

Based on our experience in Ireland, it's obvious there is no time limit to experiencing grief. Losing someone we love (a person or an animal companion) is a traumatic event that always leaves deep emotional scars. Even though I'd always intuitively known it was best for Codi to move on and leave her pain behind, this only served to temper the loss at an intellectual level. Emotionally, her death was devastating to me. While the passage of time does serve to push the pain further and further away from daily conscious awareness, certain thoughts or circumstances can arise to easily bring it back to front and center quite quickly. I found this to be particularly the case throughout the time I spent writing this book. There were numerous instances when I'd read a paragraph I'd just written and, within a second or two, I'd begin to choke up.

The undeniable truth is that my connection with Codi was so powerful there is no *getting over* her loss. For anyone who loses a beloved pet, there is only learning to live with it. What other option is there other than simply doing our best to keep moving forward and living life? None, of course, because the plain fact is, loss is part and parcel of the human experience. As I stated previously, the pain provides the contrast that allows us to more fully appreciate all of the joy we get to experience. We also derive some benefit from the loss because it serves to remind us how important it is to treasure the relationships we have with the loved ones who remain with us. In my case, there's no question the BC's passing caused me to more deeply value my connection with Andrea and with Heidi as well. In addition, thanks to Codi's admonition in Chapter 21 that "there is no tomorrow, *only now*," I've actually become somewhat more adept at living in the present.

If you, too, have experienced a deep connection with an animal companion, it's my sincere hope that you've been able to relate to many things I've written about in this work. This includes, perhaps most importantly, my somewhat controversial suggestion that dogs are, in fact, far more sentient beings than the scientific experts claim them to be.

Before leaving you, on the next page I've included a lovely free verse poem my sister-in-law Roseann wrote for us after Codi passed. If you've lost a canine or other animal best friend as well, it's my wish you also will find some comfort in these words:

Codi's Gift

How do I describe the connection that is 'us?'

You came to me as such a special gift,

smiling in your special way.

You were never there before, now you'll never be gone.

How does this happen to people?

How do we live our lives taking walks, visiting friends,
cooking dinner,

not knowing there's something yet to come

to make it all seem the more,

like the glow around a star?

Our time together was too brief for me,

and though I had to let you go,

when the sun urges me on to life,

I know instinctively you're beside me, inside me.

My arms are empty but my soul is more complete

than it was before you came,

and the lessons I learned because of you

linger in the quiet moments.

How do I describe the connection that is 'us?'

With reverence and gratitude.

— *R. Romeo-Maziarek*[9]

33. Postscript – June 2008

More than three years have passed since Codi left. Although I think of her pretty much every day, fortunately the pain of losing her has diminished considerably. In some respects, this positive outcome can be attributed to the passage of time but also playing a key role was the emotional release the writing of this book itself has served to facilitate. Performing an equally important part, however, was the caring presence of my beautiful dog, Heidi, whose contribution to the healing process has been immeasurable.

While it pains me to admit it, the truth is during the nine years-plus that both dogs lived with us, Codi usually received more attention than Heidi, primarily because she was our first dog. I'm not suggesting we didn't love Heidi, because we surely did. She just wasn't the same *kind* of dog. Seemingly, she wasn't as clever, not even close to being as intense and, clearly, obedience wasn't one of her strengths. She also barked a lot more and likewise was a risk for leaving the yard if she wasn't watched carefully. Perhaps our dear friend Rick, who also served as our trusted dog-sitter for over a decade, put it best when, several years ago, he *jokingly* nicknamed Codi as Einstein and Heidi as Jughead.

With Codi gone, Heidi finally had the opportunity to emerge from the BC's shadow. In the process, she demonstrated just how much we had underestimated her. As it turns out, in all those years while playing Codi's understudy she must have felt there wasn't any need for her to show off her own skills until she was playing a leading role! Once she assumed the position as top dog, we began to see a different Heidi appear, a much more confident dog who actually was smarter than we had ever imagined. For example, the dog which always needed to be monitored while out in the yard was replaced by a responsible canine that could be trusted outside under virtually all circumstances. The only exception being, that if another dog just happened to be walking down the street the trust part might *not* always apply! Moreover, the obstinate "little pup" that had a tendency to ignore most of our commands steadily became more obedient.

What ultimately became very obvious to me was the fact that, upon closer observation, many of Heidi's alleged weaknesses actually were her *strengths*. Her lack of focus was really the asset of being more impulsive; her laid back approach to life may have lacked intensity, but it made her more approachable; her proclivity for barking made her an incredible watch dog, despite the numerous false alarms it generated. And, her tendency to be somewhat overly affectionate at times (i.e., too much licking and jumping) was, in reality, something to be cherished, not frowned upon.

Over the past couple of years, I also came to realize that Heidi is every bit as valuable a spiritual teacher to me as Codi ever was. Her instructions include frequent reminders to be less intensely focused and more spontaneous. Her clever teaching methodology for this lesson is to first crawl under my desk while I'm working, then continuously bump her snout up against my leg until I stop staring at the monitor and begin paying attention to her. Heidi also consistently shows me how essential it is to be kind and friendly to whomever I encounter. She teaches this lesson each time we walk around the neighborhood by greeting literally every human she meets with a rapidly wagging tail and happy, high-pitched, friendly barks. Finally, every single day, she demonstrates the importance of showing love and affection to those we care most deeply about. This lesson is taught in a number of ways, my favorite one being how she'll jump up on the couch, lick me a few times on the face, then curl up right next to me and go to sleep.

As I write this in the middle of 2008, Heidi is in her 13th year. Gratefully, she continues to be very healthy and active. Although in late 2006 we decided to get another dog to keep her company and actually did bring home a Border Collie puppy at one point, after just one night with us we chose to promptly return her to the breeder. The reason was very simple: after nine years of being the "second dog," Heidi more than earned the right to have all of our attention to herself. We, therefore, do our best each day to lavish as much of it on her as we possibly can. In return, she provides us with an invaluable amount of unconditional love. There's no doubt in my mind that we're getting the better part of the bargain. She truly is an amazingly sweet and loving dog.

While we're certain that one day we'll have another dog (or dogs) to share our home, we've decided that, for the balance of Heidi's life, it will be just the three of us. Heidi, by the way, is perfectly fine with that choice!

34. *Endnotes*

1. Energy healing is based on the belief that our "life force" creates energy fields that are unbalanced during emotional or physical disease. Healers operate in many different ways. For example, they visualize, send intentions for diseased cells to die, send intentions for cells to revert to their optimum state of health, or simply send loving energy.

2. This is also referred to as the aura, the etheric body, and the etheric field.

3. For additional detail regarding this energy clearing technique, please send an e-mail to the author using the address on the Author Contact page on the following page.

4. To learn more about Canine Transfer Factor Plus visit: http://www.4life.com.

5. Produced by Pharmaloe, Aloe Vera Pet Crumbles include whole leaf Aloe Vera juice that has been shown to be effective in the treatment of the symptoms of arthritis, hip-dysplasia, chronic vomiting, gas, dull coat, and lethargy. To learn more about this supplement visit: http://www.pharmaloe.com.

6. Complete details regarding services offered by animal communicator and Reiki practitioner Pam Sourelis are located at: http://www.wingedhorsehealing.com.

7. In her first session with Codi, Pam Sourelis noted that Codi did not speak to her in direct dialog. Instead of using words, she chose to share information via her feelings that Pam was then able to intuit/pick up. In

addition, the actual process involved Pam sending Reiki healing throughout the session.

8. To learn more about Jeff Maziarek's first book, *Spirituality Simplified*, visit: http://www.spiritsimple. com.

9. Codi's Gift © 2006; Codi Image © 1994 by Roseann Romeo. All rights reserved. Reproduced by permission of the artist. E-mail: rmaziarek@hotmail.com

35. *Author Contact*

If you would care to comment or have questions regarding this book, please direct your correspondence to:

Jeff Maziarek
E-mail: codi@codipup.com

Readers are also invited to post comments regarding the book, or about their own experiences with dogs or other pets, on the *Codi's Journey* blog website at www.Codipup.com or on the *Codi's Journey* Facebook page.

Photo Gallery

From upper left:
> *First night home*
> *Settling in*
> *This clay pot is nice and cool!*
> *First trip to a park*

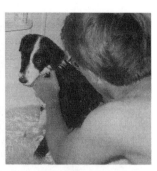

The toy obsession begins (June 1992)
First bath (July 1992)
Dad, get me out of here! (August 1992)
Don't EVER do this to me again!

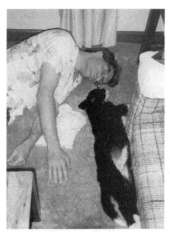

From upper left:

Tuckered out after tug of war

Leaping high to catch a tennis ball

The BC wins a wrestling match

Codi grudgingly plays along

Dad, can I have a lick of toothpaste?
Codi the Chicago Bulls Fan
Wearing visor for 20 seconds
Birthday celebration

From upper left:

In classic pose

At work

Enjoying a favorite snack

Tolerating reindeer antlers

Come on dad, it's time to get up!
In an igloo with her prized Frisbee
Entertaining in the park
Relaxing on the couch

From upper left:
   Doing what she most loved to do
   In her spot by the side of the bed
   Codi and Heidi (2002)
   Begging in the kitchen (2002)

A rare moment of pack coziness (2003)
A tug-of-war battle (2003)
Lounging on a comforter (early 2004)
October 2004 (six months after diagnosis)

From upper left:

November 2004

December 2004

Last Christmas photo together (2004)

Codi in early 2005

Two weeks before her passing (March 2005)
Sister-in-law Roseann's drawing
The "shrine" in Jeff's office
Codi's photo box/ashes with a lock of her hair

From left:

Heidi on her *couch in March 2007*
On her *bed in December 2007*

Made in the USA
Charleston, SC
10 March 2012